DATE DUE

THE
FOOD &
DRINK
POLICE

James T. Bennett
Thomas J. DiLorenzo

America's Nannies, Busybodies & Petty Tyrants

Transaction Publishers
New Brunswick (U.S.A.) and London (U.K.)

Library of Congress Catalog Number: 98-34511
ISBN: 1-56000-385-5
Printed in the United States of America

Library of Congress Cataloging-in-Publication Data

Bennett, James T.
    The food and drink police : America's nannies, busybodies, and petty tyrants / James T. Bennett, Thomas J. DiLorenzo.
        p. cm.
    Includes bibliographical references and index.
    ISBN 1-56000-385-5 (alk. paper)
    1. Political correctness—Humor. I. DiLorenzo, Thomas J. II. Title.
PN6162.B415   1998
814'.54—dc21   98-34511
                                                                    CIP

Contents

Acknowledgments

The *Food and Drink Police* was written as a critical analysis of the shrill, self-anointed scolds who want to run almost every detail of our lives—even the potato chips that we consume—by using the coercive force of government. These self-appointed national nannies, a group of pompous busybodies, are condescending, elitist, and hypocritical. The vision of the portly and oh-so-self-important C. Everett Koop, scold-in-chief, warning us to *Shape Up! America* (the name of his latest pitch group), evokes annoyance, disgust, and ridicule and reminds us of the old adage about those who live in glass houses.

We are not necessarily critical of lifestyle advice to "shape up," "eat less," "exercise more," or "everything in moderation." Far from it. This is good advice, if not common sense. What we do oppose is the use of governmental coercion through taxation, product bans, regulations, restrictions on free commercial speech, and the other authoritarian tools preferred by the busybodies whom we label the food and drink police.

Persuasion is fine—it's the American way. Coercion, compulsion, prohibition, and the trashing of civil liberties is not. This book encourages all Americans to thumb their noses at the supercilious idiocy conjured up by our self-appointed national nannies.

We gratefully acknowledge the generous support of this work by the Sunmark Foundation; the outstanding editorial assistance of Bill Kauffman, who added myriad "zingers" of his own; and the research assistance provided by John Berlau, Christopher Farris, Jeffrey Linden, and Christopher Sanderhoff. We, of course, are solely responsible for any errors.

1

Meet the Killjoys

*Socialism is nothing but the criminalization of
the pet peeves of intellectuals and agitators.*
—Anonymous

If Herbert Hoover's promise of a chicken in every pot failed to stir
the voters, imagine how little appeal a lentil (well, eight or nine lentils)
in every pot would have for Americans. Yet that is, with only a slight
caricature, the goal of one of the most media-savvy groups in all of
National Nannydom: the Center for Science in the Public Interest (CSPI).

In Richard Klein's charming cultural history of the idea of fat, *Eat
Fat*, the author, after surveying the lengths to which the nutrition Nazis
will go to regulate what goes into our mouths, concludes, "Big brother
lies at the end of the dreams of some of those who want us, at all cost,
to be healthy, slim, and beautiful."[1]

We have been inside the Washington office of CSPI, and can report
that while the health and beauty of its cadre of fat-phobic, beer-bash-
ing, Doritos-detesting, lasagna-loathing zealots may be in the eye of
the beholder, they are nothing if not slim. Virtual starvelings, or so they
seemed on the fall day that one of the authors made the trek to CSPI's
Connecticut Avenue redoubt. Scarecrows scurried here and there, grimly
clutching faxes and fact sheets that no doubt proved or at least asserted
with the basso voice of pseudo-scientific surety that whatever you are
eating at this very moment *will kill you*. And just in case any CSPI
underlings are stricken with subversive hankerings for honey-mustard
pretzels or a Hershey bar with almonds, office policy forbids the consumption of "junk food" on the job.[2] Whether employees are moni-
tored at home as well, we cannot say.

Now, there have always been and always will be ascetics, wearers of
hairshirts, self-scourgers, and in a free society they are at perfect liberty

1

to act (and eat) as their consciences (or bellies) dictate. If you wish to subsist on a diet of lentils and rice, with an occasional spoonful of gruel thrown in for a flavorful change of pace, then you are welcome to it, as long as you don't set a place at your table for the authors. But CSPI and the other busybodies who we shall examine in this book including Mothers Against Drunk Driving (MADD), which puts itself virtually above reproach by its very name, are not content to use the honorable tool of moral suasion. It is not enough for them to try to convince the rest of us to renounce the sinful acts of devouring a bacon-cheeseburger (with a hint of lettuce on top, just to placate them) or drinking a beer whilst reclining on a couch and enjoying the organized violence of a football game. For nothing angers those who are certain of their purity and rectitude quite so much as the sight of someone ignoring their advice and having a swell time. No, these folks are not satisfied with saying their piece in the marketplace of ideas. For that marketplace, like the marketplace of goods they seek to regulate, sometimes produces results that offend them. So they reach for that ever-ready cudgel of the censorious set: the coercive power of the state. Those of us unenlightened enough to live by our own lights had better toe the line.

Robert Shoffner, the tart-tongued food and wine editor of the *Washingtonian*, says of CSPI that "there's a political point of view here, an economic view based on the idea that people are children and have to be protected by Big Brother or Big Nanny from the awful free-market predators.... That's what drives these people—a desire for control of other people's lives."[3]

So just who are these people? The Center for Science in the Public Interest was founded in 1971 by a trio of Ralph Nader's self-styled consumer advocates: Michael F. Jacobson, Albert J. Fritsch, and James B. Sullivan. Jacobsen is the executive director of CSPI and its most public face: he's a slight, mustachioed man, a microbiologist with a Ph.D. from the Massachusetts Institute of Technology, a genius for attracting national publicity, and a salary and benefits package totaling about $100,000, hardly monkish.

The organization's revenues have skyrocketed over the past decade: from $414,632 in 1987 to more than $10 million six years later. At last count, the group's budget exceeded $13 million; it employed about fifty eschewers of junk food. Most of its revenue comes from direct mail—junk mail, in the common parlance—and an oddly wasteful activity for a group that professes concern for the environment, not to mention, as they phrase it, the marketing madness of our modern society.

The Center may strike an ascetic pose, but its fund-raising activities are nothing if not up to date. No standing on a street corner, begging with a tin cup for this outfit. The fastidious consumer is even urged to apply for a CSPI Gold MasterCard through MBNA America. "The only card we endorse is the only card you will ever need,"[4] states the slick brochure, which features a photograph of a CSPI MasterCard issued to someone with the preppy name of C. Bard Cole. At the top left of the photo, just above Mr. Cole's card, sits an elegantly patterned cup which is filled with what looks, to the untutored eye, to be a beverage suspiciously similar to coffee. Coffee: black heart-attack juice, the deadly diuretic. Say it ain't so, C. Bard Cole: fill that cup with a nice herbal tea.

Credit cards are most commonly used at restaurants, which in CSPI demonology are only slightly less sinister than the snake in the Garden of Eden. The Center's scruples do not extend so far as to limit the kinds of food purchases that can be charged to the CSPI Gold MasterCard: the irony is, shall we say, delicious. How many braised ribs, veal cutlets smothered in sauce, and cakes rich enough to sate Paul Prudhomme have been charged to this credit card, profiting the Center for Science in the Public Interest?

The Center's Board of Directors includes actress Anne Bancroft, who, being married to the slovenly slapstick comedian-director Mel Brooks, presumably knows a thing or two about junk food. Indeed, the board is striking for its decidedly unscientific makeup: actors are outnumbered by scientists.

Money comes from such guardians of the public weal as the Rockefeller Family Fund, the Smith Richardson Foundation, and the Streisand Foundation of Los Angeles. (An amusing funding sidelight, as reported by the *New Republic*, is that in 1982 the Center received a $38,000 grant from the Mary Reynolds Babcock Foundation of North Carolina—that's $38,000 in tobacco-grown money. Profiting from the merchants of death!)[5]

The Center's agenda is harsh neo-puritanism. Ban, restrict, end, and regulate are common admonitions in CSPI's publications. It disregards the First Amendment: billboards, television and radio advertisements, even sponsorship of events by such malefactors as Miller Brewing are to be outlawed. Beer, wine, and liquor are to be punitively taxed so that working people can no longer afford that six-pack that Michael Jacobson thinks is bad for them in the long run. "Junk" food as defined by CSPI is to be either severely regulated or banned outright; even such venerable ethnic cuisines as Chinese, Mexican, and Italian are denounced as unhealthy.

Shoffner, the restaurant critic (and a man many, many pounds this side of obese), points to the impoverishment of the CSPI ideology. "The food police," he says, "view our bodies as machines that simply need refueling with proper octane."[6] There is no sense of pleasure, of celebration, of *joie de vivre* in CSPI publications. Oh, sure, *Nutrition Action Healthletter* sometimes mentions taste, though the effort seems both half-hearted and labored. You may think you're giving up a lot in renouncing sirloin steak or creamy sauces, but hey, when it comes to mouth-watering deliciousness, there's nothing like raw legumes.

These are the folks, after all, who regard "cookies, candy, or ice cream"[7] as the bonbons of the Anti-Christ; instead of stuffing your face with such sinful confections, the *Nutrition Action Healthletter* orders the Dilberts of America to "keep a bag of peeled baby carrots on your desk."[8] Or, for those who really crave flavor and like to live on the edge, "Open and rinse a can of chickpeas or pinto beans to munch on."[9]

The joylessness of the CSPI dietary regimen is reflected in as mundanely bizarre an incident as its president Michael Jacobson eating lunch at a Chinese restaurant. As Stephen Glass of the *New Republic* describes it:

[O]rdering takes close to fifteen minutes. Jacobson, a slim, intense man, quizzes the waitress on every detail: What is the shrimp stir-fried in? And the ingredients for the sweet-and-sour chicken's breading? And precisely how many pinches of salt are added to the lo mein? The waitress, who barely speaks English, seems confused. Just before she walks hurriedly away, Jacobson blurts out a last request: Could she bring lots of extra plates? When the food comes, Jacobson examines his broccoli in brown sauce carefully. Then, picking up the platter, he maneuvers it above the first empty plate gravely, in a manner not unlike a surgeon at a particularly tricky juncture with the knife, or a priest at the moment of transubstantiation. He tips the platter just a bit, so the broccoli stays put but the sauce pours off, forming a large, brown puddle on the plate. Jacobson turns his attention to a second empty plate. Onto this, he spoons serving upon serving of white rice, and then, again with that surgico-priestly air, he slowly mixes in the denuded broccoli. The final gastronomic result is one large serving composed of about seven parts white rice to one part broccoli, all of it as thoroughly integrated as a model magnet school. His mush makes you quite suddenly lose your appetite, one of Jacobson's veteran dining companions says. "I warn you: don't order an egg roll. He'll tell you to blot off the globs of fat with your napkin."[10]

Do we, the freeborn citizens of the United States of America, really want this nut dictating our gastronomic behavior? The iconoclastic British man of letters, John Mortimer, once remarked, "I refuse to spend my life worrying about what I eat. There is no pleasure worth forgoing just for an extra three years in the geriatric ward."[11] Mortimer's preference may not be yours (it certainly isn't Michael Jacobson's) but haven't we the right to make up our own minds?

In his entertaining skewering of *The Pleasure Police*, David Shaw quotes the psychologist and advocate of "defensive" eating, Dr. Stephen Gullo, as advising his thin-obsessed patients to "drink a tomato juice before ordering" in restaurants; tomato juice, after all, is "a natural appetite suppressant." To which Shaw adds, "I assume he also advises his clients to masturbate before making love."[12]

In the harrowing world of CSPI, pleasure is suspect. These guys make Cotton Mather look like a lotus-eating, chaise-lounge-reclining sybarite. Nor is there such a thing as goofing off. Even downing a Pepsi after a strenuous workout is a virtual sin for you've consumed "160 calories of nothing. No vitamins, minerals, fiber, or phytochemicals. You just squandered an opportunity to chalk up one terrific serving of fruit...."[13]

For a group that observes the etiquette of political correctness, CSPI openly affronts people of poundage. The nascent "fat is beautiful" movement may not be everyone's cup of egg nog, but it is certainly preferable to the agenda of the Center for Science in the Public Interest, which seeks to freeze, via government fiat, the current idealization of thin as beautiful. We are witnessing an attempt to impose a tyranny of the slender: the scarecrows are sick and tired of the rest of us enjoying ourselves at mealtime, and they're not going to take it anymore. So they employ a two-track strategy: they lobby the federal government to mandate their idea of a healthy diet, and they campaign clamorously against demonized foods, pushing the not-so-subtle message that Fat Is Ugly.

Yet it was not so many years ago that Mae West was the American model of comliness; young men in the 1940s were turned on by the ample Betty Grable, not toothpick-like Kate Moss. Men of some bulk were not regarded as loathsome slobs; spindly models with the pallor of heroin junkies were not the masculine ideal. But to our nutrition nannies, sin is measured in pounds. Slimness is virtue. Eating makes people fat, and the fat are both ugly and moral lepers.

But give the Center credit: the hours that the rest of us spend eating, they devote to image-polishing. No one cultivates the electronic media like CSPI.

"Sometimes it's fun to joust with major companies,"[14] Michael Jacobson says, giving a David and Goliath twist to a personal story that bears much greater resemblance to the early twentieth-century Prohibitionist harridan Carry Nation attacking saloons with her hatchet. Take a better look at this self-styled David: the slingshot is aimed directly at *you.*

Folks who deal with Jacobson and CSPI seldom come away singing their praises:

> The problem with Jacobson is that he's like the Ayatollah Khomeini. He's an idealist. He's a zealot. There is no compromise. He is right. Everyone else is wrong.[15] (Jeff Nedelman, Grocery Manufacturers of America)

> They're really a misnomer. It's not always science, and these mini-scares are not in the public interest.[16] (Bernadine Healy, former director of the National Institutes of Health)

> They find hooks and they find gimmicks. They have a full bag of tricks that do draw attention.[17] (Roger Coleman, National Food Processors Association)

> "You know how these groups are. They...have to raise money.[18] (A "friend" of CSPI at the Food and Drug Administration)

And how better to raise money than by getting your mug on television, the great validator in our culture?

Certain of Jacobson's publicity stunts have been clever: dressing up as Tony the Tiger to protest sugary children's cereals, for instance, or chipping away with hammer and chisel at a fifty-pound block of hydrogenated fat. Newspapers and television reporters eat this stuff up: Jacobson can enliven dull dietary stories with great visuals. But these antics obscure the flimsy evidence on which CSPI puritanism is based.

The *Los Angeles Times* has reported that Jacobson directed the editorial staff of *Nutrition Action Healthletter*, the flagship monthly publication of the Center for Science in the Public Interest, to drop "weasel words"—important qualifiers such as "suggests" and "maybe."[19] How boring, how flat, how stale for an article about food X to state that it *may,* under certain circumstances and given excessive consumption, be deleterious to one's health. How much livelier, attention-grabbing, and fun to call a press conference and dress up as a giant cancer cell! And what an indictment it is of television news that Jacobson's stunts get him the air time that a real live scientist could never get. Oh, sure, the correspondent will sometimes include a five-second snippet of a rebuttal by someone identified as "an industry spokesman," but we have been conditioned to dismiss such mouthpieces as covering up for corporate malfeasance. The guy dressed as Tony the Tiger, on the other hand...what's in it for him? He's a "public advocate" or "consumer advocate," selflessly dedicating his time (and earning a pittance of a salary) to protecting you, the concerned consumer. The publicity game is rigged before the opening whistle ever blows.

What makes officious groups like CSPI so maddening is that they cloak their apparent goal—prohibition (of many things), but never by that now-discredited name—in the language of health advocacy. Some of the advice in *Nutrition Action Healthletter* is perfectly innocuous: older people should exercise. Broccoli is salubrious. (If you can stomach it.) A high-fiber diet may help prevent colon cancer. Wash your hands thoroughly after handling raw meat. It's hard to argue with any of that, and if readers heed this advice, they're liable to be healthier.

But commonsense health is only the attractive tip of the CSPI iceberg. A darker force impels this group, and all the nannies whose aseptic realms we shall visit: a combination of power-lust, the urge to coercion, and blind certitude. This last quality is on display in the career of one of Jacobson's friends. Among CSPI's sidelights is the Center for Study of Commercialism, of which Jacobson is secretary. This mini-center is devoted to "research and oppose the infusion of commercialism into practically every corner of American life";[20] its advisors include long-time auto-safety crusader Joan Claybrook. Saint Joan's track record is an illuminating study in the pitfalls of nannydom. She "was instrumental in requiring air-bag safety systems in cars,"[21] as the *Wall Street Journal* has noted. This is not exactly an untarnished accomplishment, for the National Highway Traffic Safety Administration reports that between 1989 and 1996, more than sixty people, almost forty of them children, were killed when airbags deployed in low-speed crashes. (A typical, fatal air-bag accident, which killed seven-year-old Allison Sanders of Maryland, occurred at nine miles an hour.) In addition, the NHTSA tallied an astounding 300,000 air-bag-related injuries in 1995 alone.

You would think that sixty deaths would be enough to shake the confidence of even the most cocksure nanny, but not Joan Claybrook. There is voluminous evidence that Claybrook, head of the National Highway Traffic Safety Administration under President Carter, knew of the dangers that airbags posed to children riding in the front passenger seat. General Motors Vice President Betsy Ancker-Johnson wrote Claybrook on 27 September 1979, "Through extensive development testing, we became concerned about the potential for risk of injury to unrestrained small children."[22] But Claybrook ignored these warnings. As Chrysler spokesman Jason Vines told the *Wall Street Journal*, "All along, the auto industry said, 'Hey, air bags are going to save lives, but we are concerned there are going to be some unfortunate consequences for improperly restrained occupants.' For a long time, [Claybrook] was saying, 'No way in hell are we going to open up the federal safety standard.'"[23]

What particularly galls transportation safety scholars is the arrogant and peremptory manner by which Claybrook and the auto-safety nannies imposed the air bag mandate. "In medical terms, it was like introducing a new vaccine into the marketplace with no clinical trial experiment with humans," says Harvard University School of Public Health Professor John D. Graham. "That meant the air bag became an all-or-nothing experiment with the American driver as guinea pig."[24]

Perhaps this is because Claybrook views us as lacking the faculty of reason and the freedom of choice. "The problem was that only 10 percent of the public wore seat belts," she recently told the *Washington Post* by way of explanation. "We were looking for something that was automatic [and] that didn't depend on human behavior."[25]

Human behavior. This, really, is the crux of so many of these matters. Human behavior can be unpredictable; sometimes people act in ways of which you disapprove. The mature adult accepts this; the tyrant does not, and sets out to do something coercive, and even potentially deadly, as in the air bag case, about it.

Though Claybrook is unrepentant, her fellow Naderite Clarence Ditlow, head of the Center for Auto Safety, has felt the pangs. "Maybe we share in the responsibility,"[26] he says, in the circumspect manner that passes for a *mea culpa* among these people.

You will find no such second thoughts among the busybodies at the Center for Science in the Public Interest. Point to a fatal flaw in their methodology, such as it is, and they will move on seamlessly to the next scare, never stopping to apologize to those they have wronged. As we shall see, ancient American habits—freedom of speech, liberty of action—count for nothing when nanny takes broom in hand. They have constructed a demonology as complicated as that of many religious faiths. And because it is not politic or conducive to fund raising to cast everyone in the role of the devil, they have called on villains straight from central casting: sinister corporate executives who want to make their companies and themselves rich by selling you, often under false pretenses, poisons.

The nannies are too canny to put the onus for "irresponsible" eating on the eaters themselves. They need bogeymen, and who fits that bill better than businessmen, who, as we have been taught for decades by tendentious television programs, are without exception greedy, avaricious, sneaky, underhanded white men whose ultimate goal is the destruction of life as we know it? Besides, it is easier to get the prohibitionist agenda across if it is sold as an attack on impersonal business firms rather than individuals. The economist Ludwig von Mises understood this years ago, in his opus *Human Action*: governments which are eager to keep up the outward appearance of freedom even when curtailing freedom disguise their direct interference with consumption under the cloak of interference with business. The aim of American prohibition was to prevent the individual residents of the country from drinking alcoholic beverages. But the law hypocritically did not make drinking as such illegal and did not penalize it. It merely prohibited the manufacture, the sale, and the transportation of intoxicating liquors, the business transactions which precede the act of drinking. The idea was that people indulge in the vice of drinking only because unscrupulous businessmen prevail upon them. It was, however, manifest that the objective of prohibition was to encroach upon the individuals' freedom to spend their dollars and to enjoy their lives according to their own fashion. The restrictions imposed on business were only subservient to this ultimate end.[27]

Though CSPI has its origins in the consumer movement, its publications suggest that consumers are getting too *much* for their money. Bonnie Liebman, an editor of CSPI's *Nutrition Action Healthletter*, complains that restaurants serve their customers portions that are just too darned large. To many people (but not, of course, sophisticates like herself) restaurants are "nutrition educators," says Ms. Liebman. People learn what a "serving size is by what's put in front of them." She adds, "the quantities served in many restaurants are out of control."[28]

Denny's comes in for especial condemnation. The restaurant chain gives its customers way too much food for their buck! As *Nutrition Action Healthletter* frets, "At most restaurants, Belgian waffles stand alone [phew!]. But Denny's, bless its greasy heart, will throw in *a piece of ham, two strips of bacon, or two sausage links* for about a quarter."[29] Not a bad deal for two bits, you say? Go ahead, kill yourself.

What particularly galls these erstwhile consumerists is that restaurants and fast-food joints customarily *exceed* the "official serving" size, as measured by the U.S. Department of Agriculture and the Food and Drug Administration. "We found that restaurants often serve from two to three times more than food labels list as a serving," gasps the *Nutri-*

tion Action Healthletter, with all the investigative panache of a *60 Minutes* correspondent catching fiends red-handed in the act of turning back used-car odometers. "And bigger servings mean bigger calorie, fat, saturated fat, and sodium numbers. They also mean bigger bellies and behinds."[30] They also mean better value for consumers, who are, presumably, capable of deciding how much to eat.

But in nanny's eyes, the iniquity of these overly generous restaurateurs is truly something. For example:

- The official serving size of french fries, as determined by the FDA, is three ounces but an order of McDonald's Super Size french fries is six ounces!
- An FDA official serving of popcorn is three ounces but a medium movie theater serving size is sixteen ounces! Plus you'll be adding—horrors—*butter*! And *salt*!
- An FDA official serving size of pancakes amounts to four ounces for three pancakes but restaurants typically serve four pancakes totaling ten ounces! Deport those guileful foreigners at the International House of Pancakes!
- A USDA tuna-salad sandwich serving size is four ounces but a restaurant serving is eleven ounces! ("It's as though restaurants stuff the filling from two sandwiches into one," CSPI complains.)
- A USDA official serving of sirloin steak is three ounces but "most dinner houses" serve seven-ounce steaks, and a Porterhouse may tip the scales at seventeen ounces![31]

So, not only are you too dumb to know *what* to eat, you also haven't a clue as to how *much* to eat. A smiling waiter at your local greasy spoon could serve you twenty pounds of cow dung and you'd add a little ketchup and eat it with gusto.

If you are black or Hispanic, they think even less of you. A patronizingly racist tone marks some of CSPI's material. Case in point: the Center's books, *Marketing Booze to Blacks* and *Marketing Disease to Hispanics*. We will discuss *Marketing Booze to Blacks* in chapter 3. Not since the days of Sambo and Butterfly McQueen have black Americans been so condescended to. *Marketing Disease to Hispanics* is no better. This paperback book features a preface by Congressman Matthew G. Martinez (D-Cal.) and an afterword by Rodolfo Acuña, professor of Chicano Studies, and Juana Mora, a research analyst in the Los Angeles County Office of Alcohol Programs. They provide an ethnic cover for the white boys who actually wrote the book, Michael Jacobson and Bruce Maxwell (whose surnames appear nowhere on the front or back covers).

The afterword is a classic. Acuña and Mora detect "a conscious movement" to "shift the blame to the victims by suggesting that alcohol, tobacco, and junk-food abuse is an individual choice."[32] A truly shocking discovery! Imagine: there are still Americans so lost in the fog of free will that they believe the person chugalugging a beer or swallowing a Twinkie is doing so of her own volition.

One solution is taxation: "Let's stop the sophistry and tell the people who talk about the unfair taxing of the poor to shut up!"[33] exclaim Mora and Acuña, whose grasp of such old-fashioned concepts as the free exchange of ideas seems a mite tenuous. Sure, taxing beer and cigarettes is regressive and hits the poor much harder than it does the rich, but hey: *we know what is good for you, and you had best just shut up and do it!*

The text by Jacobson and Maxwell treats Hispanics like so many five-year olds. "Diet-related health problems are tough to avoid," they write ruefully, "because we all must eat."[34] If only it were not so....

Companies that advertise such lethal products as cereal and hamburgers to Hispanic audiences come in for special condemnation. Billboards of sexy women in provocative poses are a real problem, or so we are led to believe—Latin American machismo and all that—though of course, Jacobson and Maxwell are too prissy to actually come out and say it. The authors juxtapose photos of a pretty young Hispanic woman in a Budweiser ad for the 1989 Los Angeles Cinco de Mayo festival with the next day's *Los Angeles Times* headline: CINCO DE MAYO CUT SHORT WHEN CROWDS GET ROWDY.[35] The implication is that dimwitted, oversexed Mexican-American men saw the ad, fueled up on Budweiser, and, driven crazy by the come-hither look in the model's eyes, went on a drunken rampage. Those Mexicans, you know....

Jacobson and Maxwell conclude with a call for the government (by which we assume they mean the Leviathan in Washington, DC) to ban billboards, restrict stores that sell alcohol from operating in Hispanic areas (remember, Hispanics are not smart enough to make their own shopping decisions), and "greatly increase funding"[36] for every social program under the sun.

The report did not exactly strike a chord within the Hispanic community. But then CSPI is not what you'd call a populist organization. Americans, in the millions of individual decisions they make each day, have demonstrated fairly conclusively that when they eat out, they don't want to choose off a CSPI menu. McDonald's quietly dropped the McLean Deluxe hamburger: this patty simply was no match for Chicken McNuggets or greasy french fries.

Again, an economist (and whoever dubbed the field "the dismal science" never read a nutrition textbook) comes to the defense of the burger-chomping. The Nobel laureate James Buchanan has explained why the meddlers must be stopped:

> There is an implicit recognition by all parties…that, although each may have pref-
> erences over the others' behavior, any attempt to *impose* one person's preferences
> on the behavior of another must be predicted to set off reciprocal attempts to have
> one's own behavior constrained in a like fashion. An attitude of live and let live,
> or mutual tolerance and mutual respect, may be better for all of us, despite the
> occasional deviance from ordinary standards of common decency.
>
> Such an attitude would seem to be that of anyone who claimed to hold to
> democratic and individualistic values, in which each person's preferences are
> held to count equally with those of others. By contrast, the genuine elitist, who
> somehow thinks that his or her own preferences are superior to, better than, or
> more correct than those of others, will, of course, try to control the behavior of
> everyone else, while holding fast to his or her own liberty to do as he or she
> pleases.[37]

It is testament to the decency and forbearance of those deemed fat, dissolute slobs by the nutrition and alcohol nannies that puritanical and abstemious proposals and laws have not been met by the reciprocal efforts to which Buchanan refers. No one is suggesting that Michael Jacobson be force-fed chili dogs; MADD fund-raising parties are not required by law to feature beer kegs or open bars. All we ask is that the nannies permit us to go our own way, design our own diets, and ingest what we choose to ingest. But "let me alone" is not a request to which tyrannical zealots often accede. As the following will show, this is not part of nanny's worldview.

The Constant-Crisis Mentality

What *is* a part of nanny's worldview is the notion that we are in a perpetual state of crisis, with pervasive assaults on "public" health caused by profit-hungry corporations which carelessly expose us to their "dangerous" products. As described in the coming chapters, gov-ernment regulators work hand-in-hand with many nonprofit-sector nanny groups, such as CSPI and MADD, to generate this perception of crisis. Now, we do not deny that life is risky and that there are genuine health risks from overeating, overdrinking, or unhealthy diets. But many of the health risks that the nannies harp on are bogus; and when they are genuine, the nannies' preferred "solution" is inevitably taxation, prohibition, bans on commercial speech, and other forms of authoritar-ian coercion. We citizens are not viewed by nanny as adults who can become informed about health risks and make our own decisions; our decisions must be controlled, regulated, taxed, or nullified by the self-appointed nannies and the state.

The most likely reason for all the hype created by the food and drink police is old-fashioned self-interest. As economic historian Robert Higgs showed in his classic book, *Crisis and Leviathan*, public crises have historically been the lifeblood of government.[38] Wars, depressions, or public health crises have always led to greatly enhanced power and revenues to the government, even if government fails to resolve or even alleviate the crises. And when the crisis is over, government rarely reduces its powers and revenues to pre-crisis levels. In the eyes of government bureaucrats, the worst of all crises is the absence of a crisis!

Politicians themselves thrive on crises, for crises enable them to rush in, before the cameras, and sincerely promise to "save" us all from the latest threat to our health and well-being, real or imagined. Indeed, even when there is no genuine crisis, government bureaucrats make skillful use of propaganda to create the *perception* of a crisis. As we showed in our earlier book, *Official Lies: How Washington Misleads Us*, the scope of taxpayer-funded propaganda is mind boggling.[39] For example, to exaggerate the problem of poverty, the official government statistics on "income distribution" omit taxes paid by the nonpoor, which overstates their income, while at the same time not counting cash welfare payments as part of the "income" of the poor, making them look worse off than they really are and the income distribution more unequal than it is.

The average farm family income is 140 percent of the average American family income, and the bulk of farm subsidies go to large, wealthy, corporate farm businesses. But farm subsidies are always advanced in the name of helping out ole Ma and Pa Kettle—the poor family farmers.

Since the nineteenth century the federal government has been warning the American public that we are about to run out of oil and other forms of energy any day now—unless, of course, we cede vast new powers and money to the government to "save" us from freezing to death in the dark. None of these forecasts has been even remotely accurate, but they do serve to create a sense of concern, if not panic, on the part of many citizens, who are then more inclined to acquiesce in governmental power grabs (and tax increases).

Then there are all the phony environmental crises, from alar to asbestos, dioxin, global warming, global cooling, the ozone layer, acid rain, and hundreds of other "problems" that real scientists—as opposed to the public relations flaks who work at so many of the "public interest" groups—have found to be not problems of much consequence at all.

The worst thing that can happen to any government bureaucrat is that the problem his or her agency was established to solve—reducing poverty, cleaning up the air and water, etc.—is actually solved. For then the public would begin asking why it is paying billions of dollars to address a nonexistent problem. Thus, it becomes necessary to constantly create the perception of a crisis, and to implant in the public's mind that only government can save it from the crisis.

The media thrive on government reports of health threats and crises—real or imagined—because it is the surest way to catch an audience—especially if the supposed threat is to children. In contrast, news that a supposed health hazard is really not much of a hazard after all is not considered to be news. Consequently, the American public can easily become misinformed. Writing about media coverage of the asbestos scare of the early 1990s, which led to a policy of ripping asbestos insulation out of virtually every public school building in America—despite the fact that scientists eventually concluded that the asbestos posed no health risk—Cassandra Moore observed that

> Reporters generally lack scientific expertise; they are under pressure to make their news timely, and find it easier to echo the declarations of government agencies than to check other sources. Thus only one writer bothered to dig out the facts during the panic over asbestos in the New York City school system and found, of course, that the alarm was unwarranted. His report went all but unnoticed while...the *New York Times* chose not to publish a letter from some prominent scientists that would have lessened the alarm. After all, bad news sells better than good.[40]

So as not to appear too self-serving in this endeavor—and to avoid breaking federal laws which prohibit partisan political activities on the job by government employees—government bureaucrats frequently contract out with nonprofit-sector "public interest" groups which, because they enjoy nonprofit legal status and tout themselves as selfless crusaders for "the public interest," are effective in promoting the government's agenda of crisis mongering. To oppose their political agenda is to oppose "the public interest" out of purely selfish motives! Claiming the self-defined moral high ground is one of nanny's many compulsions.

In some ways this constitutes a perversion of democracy, with government and government-funded nonprofit organizations using propaganda to manufacture and manipulate the "will of the people." It is one thing to simply provide citizens with information about healthy lifestyles; it is quite another thing to provide citizens with dubious or false information that promotes a prohibitionist agenda which, we argue, is all too often the *modus operandi* of the food and drink police.

Since government has such vast resources, whenever it enters a public policy debate on one side of an issue it has the capacity to drown out all other viewpoints. Once it decides to wage a propaganda war against any particular industry, whether it be tobacco, beer, "junk" food, or whatever, the industry is hardly capable of fighting back and winning— if indeed it chooses to do so. Because the government's regulatory powers are so vast, American businesses can hardly be said to enjoy free speech, for speaking freely in opposition to misguided government policy can lead to regulatory retribution or a dreaded tax audit.

Junk Science

The following chapters will also discuss the effects of the politicization of science—the use of "junk science" to promote certain political agendas while ignoring genuine science that may be critical of that agenda. According to the scientific method, scientific knowledge is gained through a slow process of hypothesis testing with different researchers attempting to replicate each others' results using different experimental methods and different data sets. Once a particular study can be replicated several times by peer-reviewed research, its results may become accepted as part of the wisdom of a particular field of knowledge. Even then, the "new knowledge" is always subject to challenge. In the field of economics, for example, the so-called Keynesian revolution in macroeconomic theory dominated economic thinking for forty years—from the 1930s through the 1970s—but has since been largely overthrown by both new research and world economic events. (Keynesianism had no explanation for the "stagflation" of the 1970s, for example).

More and more we see public policy driven by "studies" conducted not by credentialed and experienced research scientists but by employees of various interest-group organizations or the government itself. The studies are often not peer reviewed, and on the basis of a single study that was never replicated (and sometimes never even published), nationwide (or worldwide) headlines are grabbed announcing the "results." In such instances scientific "knowledge"—at least in the eyes of the general public—is not created by following the canons of the scientific method, but by the sheer volume of newspaper and television headlines. Bad knowledge drives out the good, to paraphrase Gresham's Law.

In a democracy citizens are susceptible to being misled by "junk science," for the average citizen tends to be "rationally ignorant," in the language of public choice theory, a subdiscipline of both economics and political science. The idea is that the typical citizen spends most of his or her time becoming informed about how best to perform his or her job, raising a family, getting the bills paid, making major and minor purchases out of the family budget, and generally taking care of *private* business.

When it comes to social policy issues, on the other hand, very few people think it worthwhile to invest sufficient time and effort to become even minimally informed about most issues—especially since there are *so many* political issues, now that government has become such a dominant force in every aspect of every American's life.

To make matters worse, much of the information citizens do absorb is self-serving propaganda presented by special-interest groups with an ideological ax to grind or by government bureaucrats themselves. Many such groups are discussed in the following chapters. They have become expert at deluging the public—and influencing public opinion—with their own points of view, even when those views are scientifically dubious. Special-interest groups inevitably dominate democratic decision making, and propaganda in the form of junk science is one of their most powerful tools of dominance.

Even much of peer-reviewed science has become corrupted by politics because so much of it is funded by government. It is not unusual for a single study published in a peer-reviewed journal to be trumpeted far and wide as *the truth*—provided, of course, that its results are politically correct. Dr. Malcom Ross, scientist emeritus at the U.S. Geological Survey, recently remarked that

> I am appalled by what I refer to as "regulatory science." Scientific investigation continually asks the question, "Is it true?" The role of science is not only to discover new facts and phenomena, but to uncover errors in previous investigations. Science is continually in the process of correcting previous work; no study is fixed in time.... Once a regulatory initiative...is introduced, the initiative persists even when new studies indicate that the premise upon which the regulation was based was incorrect.[41]

Expanded government regulation based on junk science not only deprives citizens of that much more of their personal freedom but it can also be very expensive as well, imposing millions or billions of dollars of costs on businesses and consumers, causing a loss of American jobs, and lowering living standards.

The Death of Common Sense

In 1994 attorney Philip Howard published *The Death of Common Sense: How Law Is Suffocating America*, which was on the *New York Times* best-seller list for many months.[42] The book revealed how it has become commonplace—the norm—for government regulation to seem completely detached from common sense. So much so that regulation typically imposes enormous costs—in terms of money, time, and inconvenience—on American consumers, businesses, and employees, with very little benefit, if any.

It is this kind of hairbrained, out-of-control regulation that the food and drink police champion and seek to expand, as we will show in the remainder of this book. Americans need to ask themselves if they are being well served by government policy that:

- Requires businesses to post large POISON signs on bags of sand;
- Prohibits Catholic nuns from converting an abandoned house into a homeless shelter because it does not have an elevator to service the handicapped;
- Assesses heavy fines on meat-packing plants for having "loose paint located twenty feet from any animal";
- Prohibits "habitation" in a house under renovation under the Resource Conservation and Recovery Act;
- Requires home builders to label bricks as "poisonous" and to report to the government exactly how many "poisonous" bricks are used to build each house;
- Fines restaurants for failing to put warning labels on salt;
- Imposes fines on day care centers that have cobwebs on their ceilings;
- Complains to cheese manufacturers that their walls are "too rough" and forces them to replaster and paint them;
- Requires hammer manufacturers to comply with thirty-three pages of federal regulations proscribing how hammers are to be built;
- Forces hospitals to spend 25 percent of their budgets on paperwork that merely informs federal bureaucrats of what has been going on at the hospitals; and,
- Requires certain strip joints to build wheelchair ramps just in case a handicapped stripper applies for employment.[43]

These are just a few selected examples of the kind of regulatory madness that pervades governmental decision making. If the food and

drink police are successful, we will soon be well supplied with infi-
nitely more asinine examples.

2

Eat, Drink, and Keel Over:
Lasagna, Egg Rolls, and Popcorn Can Kill

*We have to offer up scary scenarios, make
simplified, dramatic statements, and make little
mention of any doubts we may have. Each of us
has to decide what the right balance is between
being [politically] effective and being honest.*
—Steven Schneider, *Discover,* October 1987

The food police are everywhere, from the idiot box to the U.S. Cong...
well, to the other idiot box. Given that life expectancy has reached
seventy-six years, as opposed to forty-seven years in 1900, the nationwide hysteria over the mortal peril posed by Doritos and Budweiser
and a medium-rare steak seems odd; saturated fat gets worse press than
Jack the Ripper ever did. Besides, as the *Washingtonian* food and wine
editor, Robert Shoffner, notes somewhat puckishly:

> Isn't it interesting that all the culinary icons of the United States, the people best-
> known for their association with food, are thriving in what we consider advanced
> years? Julia Child is over eighty. She thinks the new puritans are ridiculous. Craig
> Claiborne is fast approaching that age. Marcella Hazan, one of the biggest-selling
> authors of Italian cookbooks, is in her seventies. They don't show any signs of
> slowing down, and they're all eating high-fat diets."[1]

We can also assume that they are not reading CSPI's *Nutrition Action Healthletter*. This monthly newsletter, the group's flagship, really
must be read to be believed. And read it is: circulation is an astonishing
800,000, and surely not every reader cherishes it for the unintentional
laughs or the gruesome photographs. (CSPI photographers can make a
simple unassuming steak sandwich look like entrails). Consider the
worldview of CSPI:

Marie Callender's frozen Pot Pies may be the most dangerous pot pies on earth (or anywhere else, for that matter).[2]

Regular Haagen-Dazs wasn't fatty enough? The folks down at Haag Central had to go and add fudge, almonds, brownies, or pecans. Guess they wanted their premium ice cream extraa faatty (perchance to mask the sweetness of each cup's nine teaspoons of sugar?). It worked. To your beleaguered blood vessels, each cup of Caramel Cone Explosion or Cookie Dough Dynamo is worse than two Big Macs.[3]

Eat an average twelve-[buffalo]wing order and you'll use up three-quarters of your day's quota for total fat, saturated fat, and sodium...plus nearly a day's cholesterol. Dip until there's nothing left of the typical bleu cheese dressing and you'll get more damaging fat than if you downed an entire Boston Market roasted chicken, *skin and all*. Even splitting an order with a friend isn't smart. (Getting an enemy to eat half is another story.)[4]

Even with nothing on the side [a mushroom cheeseburger] shoves one-and-a-half-days' worth of artery-clogging fat into your blood vessels. Get it with onion rings and you'll double the damage. Your plate's 1,800 calories will contain the fat of five strips of bacon and four Dunkin' Donuts chocolate frosted doughnuts crumbled over three slices of Domino's Hand Tossed Pepperoni Pizza, slurped down with two Dairy Queen banana splits and a Big Mac.[5]

Denny's Grand Slam is the best-selling restaurant breakfast. How can you beat two eggs, two pancakes, two strips of bacon, and two sausage links, all for $1.99?... They're grand slams all right...to your heart and waistline. We're talking more than 1,100 calories, three-quarters of a day's fat, saturated fat, and sodium, and two days' cholesterol. Cholesterol aside, that's like eating two Big Macs. If you have trouble remembering that the Grand Slam-type platter has two of everything, just think of it as the *Double Bypass*.

For an extra buck you can spring for a three-of-everything feast like Denny's *Super Slam*. Now you're talking *Triple Bypass*.[6]

It's not easy to find a food that fills up all of today's and half of tomorrow's quota of artery-clogging saturated fat. A Pizza Hut Personal Pan Pepperoni Pizza *plus* two Dairy Queen banana splits would do it. So would a single slice of The Cheesecake Factory Original Cheesecake. Yet, every year, millions order one to finish off a full dinner. Enjoy it now...it won't be on the menu at the Coronary Care Unit."[7]

And finally, of the breakfasts served at such family chains as Perkins, Denny's, Big Boy, and Bob Evans, they write:

[W]hat they serve is, generally speaking, different combinations of your arteries' worst nightmares:

- *Eggs* alone or in the waffle, pancake, or French toast batter contribute the cholesterol. *Cheese* in the omelettes adds a hefty dose of saturated fat;
- *Breakfast meats* like *bacon* and even worse *sausage* add salt and saturated fat to the wound; and
- *Margarine* on your toast, pancakes, or French toast and *shortening* in the grill grease supply saturated and *trans* fat. Both give your blood cholesterol a jolt. If your restaurant uses butter or a butter-margarine blend, it's even worse.

Any one of those ingredients is enough to make your blood vessels quake. Pile two or more on the same plate and you could be in real trouble. It's surprising that restaurants don't sell life insurance right on the premises.[8]

Butter, eggs, buffalo wings, even the diffident pot pie each could qualify as the title character in the Jim Thompson novel *The Killer Inside Me*. But what else do we learn from this perusal other than noting a curious undercurrent flowing through *Nutrition Action Healthletter*: Eat Big Macs! They're not so bad for you!

The ovophobia displayed by CSPI is simply...cracked. Eggs "in particular have gotten a bad rap," says George Washington University nutrition expert Dr. Wayne Callaway. "They're highly nutritious and, for most people, pose no health risk at all."[9] Medical studies have found that young men and women who eat three or four eggs a day (yes, a *day*) experience very modest and perfectly safe increases in their cholesterol levels. The American Heart Association says that even those on cholesterol-lowering diets can eat four eggs a week.

Walter C. Willett of the Harvard School of Public Health marvels, "You'd think there were half a dozen studies saying to avoid eggs. Guess how many there were? When we started looking at this question, zero. Now there's still very little information."[10] And yet, as Philip E. Ross pointed out in *Forbes*, U.S. egg consumption has fallen from 402 eggs per capita in 1945 to 238 today.

The poor egg, maligned for years, is finally showing its sunny side. Nutritionists praise it as an inexpensive source of protein and iron that is also low in fat and calories. "There are people who could benefit from eating more than four eggs a week," says Dr. Callaway, "the elderly, people with low incomes, and people who are not active who need nutrient-dense foods."[11]

So what, is it suggested, should the conscientious *Nutrition Action Healthletter* reader eat? He may take the "Tip of the Month," which typically reads: "Asparagus season is here. Break off and discard the woody ends, bring the stalks to a boil and steam for just two to three minutes, sprinkle with fresh lemon juice, and...and that's it!"[12]

So simple! So nutritious! So utterly flavorless! This is self-denial without the religiosity, without any elevating motive, really, beyond a drearily utilitarian view of the human body. But then these are the people who earnestly recommend that you scrape the salt off of pretzels, lest you get "a nice shot of sodium."[13]

Meanwhile, Peter Shaw notes, with Shavian wit, that a friend points out "that the greatest 'correlation' involving cholesterol is that between *low* cholesterol and highly violent behavior. So don't invite anyone with low cholesterol to dinner; he might stab you with a butter knife."[14]

The Assault on Multicultural Cuisine

In the early 1990s, CSPI mandarins aimed their scattershot fire at new targets: the increasingly popular ethnic cuisines. The highest-profile victim was Chinese food. Now, one might expect that the rice-based dishes that dominate Chinese menus would be hailed as positively ambrosial by Michael Jacobson and company, but no. Those intrepid diners who cross the threshold of the local Hunan eatery are taking "a wok on the wild side,"[15] as the *Nutrition Action Healthletter* put it.

The Center's Juliann Goldman coordinated the Chinese-food study. She and her assistants bought "take-out portions of fifteen popular dishes from twenty mid-priced Chinese restaurants in Washington, DC, Chicago, and San Francisco."[16] They shipped these fragrant packages to a lab, where the contents were vetted for calories, fat, saturated fat, and sodium—the four horsemen of the nutrition apocalypse.

The results: moo shu pork came off as a cross between arsenic and Charles Manson. Kung pao chicken led the fat parade, with an "outrageous seventy-six grams."[17] (Szechuan shrimp and stir-fried vegetables earned the encomium "respectable," fat-wise.) But even good old stir-fried vegetables flunked the sodium test: the dish graded at 2,153 mg, "about your quota for a day."[18] Other dinners ranged as high as 3,460 mg of sodium (house lo mein). "The average Chinese dinner," the authors warn, "contains more sodium than you should eat in an entire day."[19] At least most dinners were low in saturated fat with the exception of that demonic delicacy, moo shu pork.

But moo shu pork is saved from complete ignominy by the egg roll, which ranks fifteenth in CSPI's survey of fifteen Chinese dishes. "Roll it in a napkin"[20] to sop up the grease, the authors advise, in the same tone a parent might use in counseling a promiscuous teenager to use a condom. Again, the portions are just too darned large, complain these consumerists. A Chicago restaurant "gave us a pound"[21] of beef in its beef with broccoli: How dare it be so generous!

Is there no way to survive the kitchen of death known as a Chinese restaurant? In fact there is: eat "two orders of rice for every entree."[22] This may be dauntingly flavorless; why not just skip the entree and order the rice? (That's pretty much what Michael Jacobson does when he eats out.)

Its release heralded by the usual bells and whistles (though Jacobson wisely refrained from dressing as a fried wonton), the CSPI Chinese food study had its desired effect: Chinese restaurant owners in the Washington, DC area reported that business was off by 20–25 percent in the immediate aftermath. But unlike bigger businesses, which often cower or appease when struck by negative publicity, the Chinese restaurateurs struck back. "They're what I call 'extremists,'"[23] said Stephen Lee, a spokesman for DC-area Chinese restaurants. Lee charged that the focus on sodium, fat, and calories obscured the richness of Chinese dishes in fiber, vitamins, and minerals. "If it's not healthy food, then why are so many Chinese coming here?" asked Tony Cheng, owner of the much-praised Tony Cheng's Mongolian Restaurant in Washington. "Chinese people know what's good and bad."[24]

The CSPI study of Chinese food was fatally flawed, as Robert Shoffner notes with amazement:

> From their attack on Chinese restaurants, the only conclusion the public could reach is that all Chinese restaurants serve unhealthful food. There were no distinctions made. What they did was grab X number of restaurant samples…of moo shu pork, and instead of testing them individually, they threw them all in a blender and analyzed the fat content…. When I had a CSPI representative on my radio show, I asked him, Tell me, have you ever eaten in a Chinese restaurant that served greasy food? He said yes. Then I asked, Have you ever eaten in a Chinese restaurant where the food is so drained of oil you can't tell it's fried? He answered yes. Well, I said, if you throw all the samples in the blender, how can you possibly judge the good from the bad?…He said that was the way the government tests the content of various foods which tells us something about the value of government tests.[25]

The methodological flaws of this study either never made the papers or were buried on page C-24. The damage was done. Millions of Americans heard of this hit job, whether on television or radio, or in the paper, and so whenever a spouse or friend says, "Let's eat Chinese tonight," a little alarm rings, and our health-conscious consumer hesitates, a vague unease rising within, and says, "Nah, why don't we try… Mexican?"

But if Chinese chefs are, in the mythos of the Center for Science in the Public Interest, inscrutable, the Mexicans are incorrigible. The CSPI morality play casts Mexican chefs in roughly the same role as the corrupt lawmen in John Huston's film *The Treasure of the Sierra Madre*: one can imagine them growling, "Nutree-tion? We don't need no stinking nutree-tion."

Again, the CSPI methodology was suspect. As with the Chinese study, CSPI factotums braved nineteen temples of fat in Chicago, Dallas, San

Francisco, and Washington, DC and purchased take-out portions of fifteen dishes, threw nine samples of each dish into what amounted to a sloppy specimen jar, and had it tested by a laboratory for calories, fat, saturated fat, cholesterol, and sodium.

Given the ubiquity of rice and beans in Mexican cuisine, one might think that the gringos at CSPI would give it a supercilious tip of the sombrero. But no.

Mexican food is so spectacularly wicked that we are advised to eat (if we must eat) at Chinese restaurants. After all, the fastidious diner can always gorge himself on "steamed rice" and eat "half of whatever comes with it." The rice at the typical Mexican restaurant, by contrast, contains more than 800 milligrams of sodium per serving. The beans are almost as bad—some have been adulterated by lard, bacon, or even gasp! cheese!

As usual, common dishes are maligned as somehow less healthy than absurd quantities of junk food. An order of beef and cheese nachos, we are told, has "as much fat as ten glazed doughnuts at Dunkin' Donuts."[26] A chile relleno supplies the unwitting nibbler with "as much saturated fat as twenty-seven slices of bacon."[27]

Sour cream and guacamole do not make the most salubrious daily menu but is there a person alive who exists solely on a sour cream-guacamole diet? There is absolutely no evidence—none—that an occasional night out at a Mexican restaurant is harmful to your health. On the other hand, hypochondria demonstrably *is* harmful.

Chicken fajitas got a grudging thumbs-up: "there's not much you can do to ruin strips of marinated skinless chicken breast,"[28] they concede, and note how condiments, sauces, spices, and other piquant contributors to gustatory pleasure are lumped into the "ruin" category. One small restaurant chain in the Northwest (Macheezmo Mouse) was praised for its menu, which includes such customer magnets as steamed broccoli, non-fat yogurt, and no-fat black beans and, presumably, straps over the chairs to keep diners from leaving after they see the menu.

The soft chicken taco gets a qualified recommendation because "they're so small, tacos are pretty good fat bargains."[29] The message: if you must eat Mexican, don't eat.

Okay, so Mexican is out. "How about eating Italian tonight?" our vigilant watcher of saturated fat and calories asks. To which CSPI responds, "Are you nuts?" After all, fettucini Alfredo is "a heart attack on a plate;" don't order it unless "your cardiologist is on call."[30] Eggplant parmigiana is as bad as "five egg rolls."[31] (Chinese is as bad as Mexican is as bad as Italian is as bad as Chinese....)

Yes, spaghetti won't kill you, and if you must, if you really must, you can dress it in tomato sauce (meatless, please), but anything else is the digestive equivalent of flipping Don Corleone the bird. "Skip the cheese"[32] goes CSPI's tasteless tip after its comprehensive mini-paragraph summary of the most loved Italian dishes.

All right, so Italian is out. As is Mexican and Chinese. Let's just go to a movie. Maybe buy a big tub of popcorn, every nutritionist's favorite snack. Just sit back in the plush chairs of the local multiplex and stuff our faces with fiber-rich...*artery-clogging fat*!

Yes, movie lovers, not only are you blowing seven bucks on a silly movie when you could be home cleansing your lentils, but those tubs of yellowy popcorn you and your sweetie buy are clogging your arteries thicker than a 5:15 Beltway traffic jam. Squirt some butter atop a large order and "the heart-unhealthy fat is equal to nine McDonald's Quarter Pounders."[33] (There they go again. Are these people Ray Kroc's heirs or what?)

And at the end of all this worrying, all this sodium measuring and calorie counting and other dreary tasks, the wise woman orders whatever the hell she wants to order and tapes to her refrigerator the sage advice of Mark Twain: "Part of the secret of success in life is to eat what you like and let the food fight it out inside."[34]

Or as a gang of guerrilla gourmands calling themselves Devour stated after one CSPI report: "We don't want to eat sawdust, and we reject the gustatory nannies attempting to shove their bland, boring, ascetic lifestyle down our throats." Devour warned, "No amount of fruit, vegetables, legumes, ginseng extract, bee pollen and good karma is going to save them from the Grim Reaper."[35]

Just maybe, as in Woody Allen's film *Sleeper*, many of those things that are "bad for us" will turn out to be life-savers. Chocolate, caffeine, even the junkiest sweetener: the juries are still out on the health effects of many varieties of Bad Food. Of chocolate, Sheila Lavery notes: "Apparently, women need chocolate as well as other foods that are high in starch, sugar, and fat to control weight, stabilize moods, and revitalize well-being. Indeed, failing to satisfy these needs can lead to overeating, feelings of fatigue, frequent mood swings, debilitating premenstrual and menopausal symptoms, and uncontrollable food cravings."[36] (Rather like Peter Shaw's cholesterol-deprived knife-wielders?)

Fish, depending on which study one believes, is either a piscine balm to the heart or a washout. Kids who eat a candy bar go into "sugar high" frenzies, dancing around the room; no, the "sugar high" is pure canard. In the *New England Journal of Medicine* in 1994, editors Marcia Angell and Jerome Kassirer wrote that Americans "increasingly find themselves beset by contradictory advice," for "no sooner do they learn the results of one research study than they hear of one with the opposite message."[37]

Even the Center for Science in the Public Interest countenances the consumption of seafood of the right kind, of course. "Seafood is remarkably low in (heart-damaging) saturated fat," the food cops allow. "And it's the richest source of omega-3 fatty acids, which could protect against heart attacks."[38]

But there's a fly in the ointment, as always: cramps, nausea, vomiting, and that CSPI oldie but goodie, diarrhea, lurk inside every shellfish. And "fried seafood is even high in *artery-clogging fat*."[39] Whatever you do, don't "get it stuffed or smother it in cheese, cream, butter, or tartar sauce."[40] If you really must eat out be sure to limit your side dishes to "a plain baked potato, an undressed salad...and a couple of unbuttered rolls."[41] And don't you dare order the fried seafood combo: the CSPI's patented "buy a mess of take-out portions and throw it all in a blender and see what we get" research method revealed the combo to be a virtual Everest of fat. Indeed, "add tartar sauce and the fat's equal to thirty-two Chicken McNuggets."[42] Or dip your fried clams in tartar sauce and "you end up with about as much fat as five medium orders of McDonald's French fries."[43] (Again, a subliminal voice seems to whisper: Eat McDonald's; Eat McDonald's.)

You may recall that in the early 1980s fish oil was celebrated as a virtual fountain of health. Researchers found extraordinarily low rates of heart disease in Greenlandic Eskimos, and if it works for the Eskimos.... Well, the fish oil story turned out to be just another fish story. Subsequent studies of Europeans and Americans showed, in some cases, lower rates of heart disease among fish eaters than among fish abstainers. Other studies found no link. And what about the Eskimos? As Martijn Katan, a scholar from the Netherlands, explained, "In studies of Eskimos who, incidentally, ate seal and whale rather than fish, low rates of coronary disease were found. But their diet and lifestyle were quite special and most of them died before reaching middle age."[44]

Ooops. They didn't die of heart disease because they died of other things before reaching the typical heart-attack age.

So eat your fish if that's your wish, but do so because you love the taste, not because it's a life-saver. As even CSPI points out, aspirin is a better bet for reducing the risk of clotting, and the vaunted fish-oil capsules that were said to be a magic anti-cholesterol bullet are may be no more effective than the pills peddled by itinerant quacks of the patent-medicine age.

Whew! We Need a Cup of Coffee!

Coffee, for a time, had its reputation in the noose, but a drink that 80 percent of Americans enjoy every morning, including members of the prosperous professional class that donates money to CSPI, cannot be demonized as easily as, say, tobacco. Besides, even the most astringent observers give coffee a clean (if teeth-yellowing) bill of health.

Though it may seem to make the heart race, it won't make it crash. "There doesn't seem to be any relation [between coffee and heart disease]," says Harvard School of Public Health researcher Meir Stampfer, "even with five cups a day, and even for people who already have heart disease. To my mind, it's basically a dead issue."[45]

One 1981 study never duplicated linked coffee to pancreatic cancer. Perhaps half of all pancreatic cancers are linked to java, the authors conjectured, with the imprimatur of the prestigious *New England Journal of Medicine*. Five years after the original study, the authors conceded that such a link may not exist, but the damage had been done. Coffee, the morning ritual of tens of millions of Americans, would forever after be regarded as somehow unhealthy, as potentially dangerous. (Constant craving of coffee even has a name now—caffeine dependence syndrome. No doubt lawsuits by the CDS-afflicted are at this very moment being readied under the aegis of the Americans with Disabilities Act.)

Even CSPI, of all places, gives a cup of joe a reluctant okay. *Nutrition Action Healthletter* quotes John Weisburger of the American Health Foundation as saying that "there's no good evidence that coffee has any role"[46] in the development of bladder, breast, colon, lung, or prostate cancer.

CSPI might have gone so far as to say that a caffeine buzz is actually good for you. It improves reaction time and even athletic performance (though it is also a diuretic; so a player should be careful lest he make an ungraceful exit from the game.) Researchers at the Johns Hopkins Medical Institutions found that consumption of four cups of regular coffee per day by 100 men aged twenty to sixty raised their "good" cholesterol, HDL, as well as their bad cholesterol, LDL. These increases "should not affect coronary heart disease,"[47] according to study author Roy E. Fried.

Peter Shaw urges us not to lose ourselves in grim accounting; sure, he writes, caffeine speeds the heart and acts as a diuretic, among other things, but it "has also been reported to help people lose weight, to improve hand-eye coordination, to increase tolerance for exercise, to promote alertness and clearer thinking, to diminish drowsiness, to combat migraine headaches, to make children more attentive in school, and to make adults less likely to suffer bronchial asthma or commit suicide."[48] And isn't an extra trip to the boys' or girls' room a day worth being a keen lover of life?

Who can possibly keep track of the yo-yoing fortunes of foods? The beta carotene in carrots wards off cancer and heart disease. Everybody knows this; men and women from Seattle to Bangor are choking down raw carrots like monks pulling on hairshirts. But wait...the latest studies find beta carotene "completely ineffective in preventing cancer or heart disease."[49] Butter disappears from American tables, as saturated fat was banished until a Harvard research team, which included Dr. Walter Willett, found that the trans fats used to make margarine may be responsible for 30,000 heart-disease deaths each year. Margarine sales fell 8.2 percent the next year. Salt raises your blood pressure. But then why don't low-salt diets reduce blood pressure?

The Good News about Junk Food

Perhaps the most startling of the "that's *good/bad* for you?!?!" stories appeared in 1996, when researchers at the National Center for Health Statistics hypothesized that the reason for the falling rate of heart disease is not only exercise and better eating but the artificial flavorings in junk food. Candy, ketchup, pudding, and pop: the four new food groups for health-conscious eaters.

The heart-friendly element in many artificial flavors appears to be salicylates, which are related to aspirin, which helps prevent blood clots. The average American consumes the equivalent of a baby aspirin a day in salicylates. The artificial flavoring boom occurred in the mid-1960s coincident with a fairly steep decline in deaths due to heart disease. Dr. Manning Feinleib, one of the authors of the study, explained, "The decline in heart disease started rather abruptly in the mid-1960s. Within about three or four years it spread across the country. It's hard to imagine that something like cholesterol lowering or blood pressure treatment could explain it."[50]

(A diet tip for the heart-smart: those flavors that most often contain salicylates are strawberry, grape, butter, vanilla, cinnamon, mint, caramel, and walnut. *Bon appetite!*)

Sometimes the din grows so deafening, the cacophony so confusing, the only thing an American can do is...eat to his heart's content. "I don't want to look at another article telling me what's good and bad for me," twenty-five-year-old Hidoshi Wald told the *Washington Post* as he sipped a martini. "First they say red wine's bad. Then red wine's good. I'm going to eat red meat and make my own health decisions. I'm sick of people telling us what to do."[51]

Consumption of hamburgers, French fries, high-fat cheeses, and super-premium ice cream (the kind with the most butterfat) is rising sharply as the 1990s turn the corner toward home. James Whorton, a professor of medical history at the University of Washington, sees the first signs of a backlash against the nannies. "There's been so much emphasis on not eating fat, drinking moderately, exercising. I think people are running out of patience. We are becoming cynical. We are revolting against the self-denial."[52] And against the bad science and oversold promises, as well. For despite the "Eat Right" mania of the last twenty-five years, there is no real evidence that dietary changes as opposed to, say, medical advances account for declines in the rates of death from cancer and cardiovascular disease. As Professor Eric Rimm of the Harvard School of Public Health says, "The studies looking at fat and risk of heart disease are inconsistent. Fat is a complicated issue because there are so many types.... No one has really done a study to find out how much heart disease is due to genetics and how much to other factors."[53]

Oh, great: ten years of eating non-fat cottage cheese and for nothing!

At long last, Americans are revolting against low-fat and fat-free "foods." The percentage of people reporting that they ate at least one no-fat or low-fat item during a two-week period fell from a high 95 percent to 86 percent, according to one survey.[54] Help may be just over the horizon, in the form of Olestra but more on that in chapter 6.

Should You Try To Cut Your Gut?

At least there's one thing we can all agree on, right? And that's that fat people suffer from an entire complex of diseases brought on by obesity. 'Tis better to be thin than fat. Right?

Wrong.

Glenn A. Gaesser, a professor at the University of Virginia and associate director of the university's adult fitness program, writes in *Big*

Fat Lies, "There is a large and ever-growing body of scientific evidence, most of it still confined to professional journals, showing that fat may not be so bad, and in fact thin may not be so good."[55]

Confined to professional journals is right. We picked several diet books at random from the shelves of the local bookstore and found that the common denominator, the one point on which the feel-good, you-can-do-it authors agreed with the hectoring, stop-stuffing-your-fat-mouth drill instructors, is that obesity is just another way to commit suicide in public.

In *Think Yourself Thin*, Debbie Johnson after warning readers, "Don't loan [this book] to a friend while you are still in the first weeks of thinking thin. Tell her to get her own copy (through bookstores nationwide.),"[56] declares: "Most of us know there are health risks in being overweight. The most obvious are heart disease, high blood pressure, lessened ability to exercise, and of course negative psychological effects. The not-so-obvious risks are hypertension, some types of diabetes, and breast cancer."[57] Most of us may know this, but then most of us are wrong.

Johnson also claims that "upward of 62 percent of all North Americans are clinically obese,"[58] an outlandish figure and a nice example of wishful thinking: a nation of 155 million fatsos would constitute an enormous market for books by thinness gurus. (Two American researchers at the Baylor College of Medicine published a tongue-in-cheek piece in the *Lancet*, a leading British medical journal, claiming that by the year 2230, every adult American would be overweight. They were kidding but don't be surprised to see the joke turn up, retailed as fact, in future diet books.)

Johnson is by no means alone in diet land. The married duo of Marilyn Diamond and Dr. Donald Burton Schnell, in their cutely named *Fitonics for Life*, allege, "Every year 400,000 Americans die prematurely from cigarette smoking. But few people realize that obesity is directly responsible for over 300,000 untimely deaths during the same time period, placing excess body fat second only to smoking as a cause of preventable death."[59]

"We are literally killing ourselves as we tuck in our napkins," Diamond and Schnell gasp. "Our wounds are inflicted with knives and forks."[60] Salvation is at hand, however: just buy Nabisco Mini-Shredded Wheat with bran and, if you're in an adventurous mood, "toss in some raisins and banana, pour on the soy milk,"[61] and chow down, epicure. If soy milk on shredded wheat with bran doesn't tickle your tastebuds, some diet docs are more liberal: in *Eat Right Live Longer*, Neal Barnard gushes, "Many people think of legumes as the savory replacement for meat in their diet."[62]

In the *Redux Revolution*, Sheldon Levine tolls the knell: "Being as little as twenty-two pounds over your high school weight puts you at risk for early mortality."[63] But never fear, Sheldon is here, with his prescription weight-loss medication. Indeed, in its first nine months on the market doctors wrote 3.3 million prescriptions for Redux; another 18 million are written annually for fenfluramine and phentermine, also known as fen-phen. Yes, dear tub o' lard, you can look like the Cindy Crawford in the mirror if you'll just pop this little appetite suppressant. Why exercise when a pill enables you to shed that excess weight?

But taking the cake literally is Adele Puhn, author of the *5-Day Miracle Diet*. In her acknowledgments, she writes, "My apologies and thanks to my loving children...who endured...vitamins and Twinkie-less parties, for Halloweens with raisins and natural whole grain cookies instead of the sugar-coated, chocolate-dipped ones they would rather have had. But I now delightfully reap the rewards of having fostered this nutritional awareness when I see my three-year-old granddaughter Charlotte munch on carrot sticks instead of lollipops."[64]

Some indulgent grandma she is. Puhn deprived her children of sweets because of her belief that sugar caused hyperactivity—too bad that just as her book was being released, researchers were exploding the myth of the "sugar high." All those cookies uneaten; the poor raisin children.

Puhn's attitude and that of the entire thin-at-all-costs crowd, from the Center for Science in the Public Interest to the portliest diet doctor is encapsulated in her story of one client, an accountant in his late fifties. This fellow, who had lost twenty-two pounds, was attending a family gathering. "His favorite aunt was there with open arms. 'There you are! You look great! And guess what? I've made your favorite chocolate cake.'"[65]

Most of us would be pleased to see our favorite aunt, grateful that she had baked a cake for us, and we'd eat a piece. Not Puhn's accountant. She writes: "He did not stop to think. He could not escape...he didn't have a clue as to how to deal with his aunt and her cake.... He not only ate one piece, he ate three pieces unable to enjoy one single bite. With every forkful of cake he felt rage at his aunt and at himself. He didn't even love the chocolate cake! It was a myth perpetuated by the family to make his aunt feel loved and admired."[66]

The weight-loss-at-any-cost ethos cannot even take into account an elderly aunt's feelings. By baking a cake for her darling nephew she has become the enemy, the target of his "rage." This guy needs help.

He is in the grip of what Phillip M. Sinaikin and Judith Sachs term "fat madness"; to wit, "Fat Madness is an intense, all-consuming preoccupation with body weight, size, shape, food, and dieting. It's based on a distorted perception of yourself, a vision perpetrated by society and history and the media. Television shows, movies, and the multibillion-dollar diet industry image-makers have promised you a quick fix, if only you'd change your body. The propaganda we're all fed daily has succeeded in draining overweight people and people who just think they're overweight of their sense of self-worth and personal effectiveness."[67]

After all, a low-fat or no-fat diet won't slow aging, no matter what the starvation and treadmill gurus say. *You're going to die anyway.* Aging is not a disease, it is a natural process, and trying to forestall it by substituting legumes for beef is a silly waste of effort and taste foregone.

The diet industry racks up $30–$40 billion in sales each year—books and pills and diet soft drinks and exercise spas in which you can embarrass yourself watching impossibly muscular people effortlessly do lifts and bends which would put you in intensive care. You can't quarrel with exercise though a brisk walk does nicely, and you don't have to pay a monthly fee for the privilege but the rest of that $40 billion may be the biggest waste of money since Kevin Costner got the keys to *Waterworld.*

For poundage, it turns out, is not the death sentence that C. Everett Koop, *Nutrition Action Healthletter,* and the rail-thin nags of the diet world have told us it is.

The rethinking of "fat" has been underway for several years now; it has even made the cover of *Newsweek,* always a sign that the worm of conventional opinion is turning. Much of the credit goes to Stephen N. Blair, senior scientific editor of the Surgeon General's Report on Physical Activity and Health, who hangs his hat at Dallas's Cooper Institute for Aerobics Research, and the University of Virginia's Glenn A. Gaesser.

In his pathbreaking book, *Big Fat Lies* (1996), Gaesser writes that he was a typical "obesity is a disease" worrywart until he noticed that "the health and vigor of many heavier-than-average men and women I encountered over the years—some in the laboratory, some in my clinical experience—seemed to defy the dire warnings."[68]

Among the most striking works of research that fortified Gaesser in his new opinion was produced by Blair, who wrote the foreword to *Big Fat Lies*. Blair's eyes were opened by a study he helped direct of more than 12,000 men at high risk for heart disease. Contrary to what everyone expected, "weight loss did not lower the death rates of these high-risk men," writes Blair. "In fact, compared to men whose weights remained reasonably stable over the six to seven years [of the study] (even if those weights were *above* the recommended range), men who lost weight actually had a *greater* risk of dying during the nearly four years of follow-up."[69]

Such findings recur again and again. Gaesser reports that from 1983 to 1993, fifteen studies showed "weight loss to increase risk of premature death by up to 260 percent,"[70] yet do you happen to recall a spate of "Thin Kills; Bulk Up to Save Your Life" stories in the popular press? Of course not. Fat is the enemy, and has been for much of this century, despite such contrarians as Woods Hutchinson, one-time president of the American Academy of Medicine, who told *Cosmopolitan* readers in 1984: "Adipose, while often pictured as a veritable Frankenstein, born of and breeding disease, sure to ride its possessor to death sooner or later, is really a most harmless, healthful, innocent tissue."[71]

In the nineteenth century a few extra pounds were regarded as wise protection against two of the era's great killers, tuberculosis and pneumonia, but as other illnesses have donned the mantle of the Red Death, fat has come to be seen as a sign of sloth, sluggishness, and an early death. Dr. George Mann, writing in the *American Journal of Public Health* in 1971, rounded up the suspects in the character assassination of good old adipose: "The evil view of obesity has come from four places, the insurance industry, the medical moralizers (usually themselves thin), the drug industry and the docile, unquestioning nutritionists who are too often dupes of the faddists and hucksters."[72] Gaesser adds to this list the fashion industry and the fitness, not fatness, fanatics.

Their disapproving stares are all around us. C. Everett Koop, careening from nanny cause to nanny cause with the gleam of moral certitude in his eye, claimed at a White House ceremony with Hillary Rodham Clinton that obesity can be blamed for a thousand deaths a day. Is it any wonder that as many as a quarter-million liposuctions are performed each year? Or that perhaps 80 million Americans are dieting at any given time, even though 90 percent of them are yo-yo dieters: They go up and down, up and down, take it off and then put it back on again. "The ideal now is a body that's so thin it can't menstruate, it's infertile,"[73] says journalist Laura Fraser, author of *Losing It*, an entertaining tour of the diet-quackery industry. Fraser notes that despite the billions we spend each year on these nostrums, over the last decade the average American has gained eight pounds.

To have a full-blown "crisis" we need to concoct phony numbers, and the fat-phobes have done so. The American Obesity Association (they're anti, not pro) claims that obesity "costs" the United States $100 billion annually. As Fraser notes, one-third of this figure includes the diet industry, and part of the remainder is built on the erroneous assumption that obesity causes premature death. As we shall see in the next chapter, this has long been the practice of the prohibitionists: it's not enough to call alcohol the demon rum, you have to "prove" that this demon is ruining the economy.

Yet fat is not the enemy of fit. "Obesity is a neutral factor in matters of health,"[74] writes Glenn Gaesser. The evidence is startling; almost everything the casual dieter "knows" to be true is wrong or dubious.

For instance, "Men and women medically classified as overweight who exercise regularly and are physically fit, yet remain above the ranges recommended by the height-weight tables, have lower death rates than thin men and women who do not exercise and are unfit, and have death rates comparable to thin and average-weight men and women who do exercise and are fit."[75]

So obesity doesn't kill you. Trying to shed those pounds in a reckless manner could, though. "Weight loss does not necessarily improve health. Dieters, especially yo-yo dieters…have a risk for cardiovascular disease that is up to twice that of 'overweight' people who remain fat."[76] Fat may in fact *protect* one's health; it can guard against "cardiovascular disease and type- II diabetes, especially in women, and possibly breast and endometrial cancer as well."[77]

The mounds of new research that have buried the old "get fat and die" dogma have left many scientists scratching their heads. Those who lose weight "show an improvement in risk factors, but they die," according to Dr. David Garner, director of the Toledo Center for Eating Disorders. "I don't think that's a good outcome."[78]

In his study of the relationship between weight and longevity in the United States and Europe, Dr. Reubein Andres, clinical director of the National Institute on Aging, found that losing weight, even in modest chunks, is associated with earlier mortality. "There's every reason to expect that truly obese people would benefit from losing weight," says

Andres, "but if you look at survival, not at individual risk factors, those that lose do badly. We don't understand why."[79]

As Peter Shaw reports, a 1995 study found that even for those past seventy years of age, "the risk is not there" if one is twenty pounds overweight; health risks "begin to rise" for those over seventy only if they carry more than fifty pounds of avoirdupois. On the other hand, the "risk of mortality [is]...high in elderly people who are underweight, rising sharply the leaner they are."[80]

The scare stories are designed to frighten otherwise healthy people into fad diets. Meanwhile, cutting-edge research has shown "that there is no connection between fat-clogged arteries and obesity. Fat in the arteries and fat on the body are different and unrelated."[81] There is no evidence repeat, no evidence that atherosclerosis, the top cause of death in the United States, is caused by obesity.

Indeed, "even massively obese men and women show no connection between obesity and vascular disease," according to two researchers at the National Institutes of Health who examined the autopsies of men and women who had tipped the scales at between 300 and 500 pounds found that "there was no more atherosclerosis in their coronary vessels than in non-obese people of the same age."[82]

Gaesser counts up to forty recent studies indicating "a lower rate of cancer, and of mortality from cancer, at higher body weights."[83] This is particularly true of lung and breast cancer, as well as osteoporosis, or deterioration of the bones.

But what about hypertension, you ask: surely the facts are in, and the facts are grim for all but the thin. Well, no. Although "in obese people [hyptertension] only marginally increases the risk of premature death," quite "the reverse applies to both non-obese and thin people, for whom hypertension more than doubles the risk of premature mortality."[84] Maybe it's better for a thin hypertensive to pack on a few pounds than for a fat one to lose a bunch.

And so all that sound and fury emanating from the diet-or-die crowd may signify no more than their desire to liberate you from your hard-earned cash. Laura Fraser who at 5'6" tips the scales at 155 pounds, has a cholesterol level of 135, and rides mountain bikes for fun recommends, "use the money you'd spend on all that diet stuff to buy good walking shoes, a series of yoga classes, a bike, a cooking class, or something else that will genuinely make you feel good or improve your health."[85] (Or just stay right where you are: after all, as Sally Smith, executive director of the National Association to Advance Fat Acceptance, says, "couch potatoes have rights, too."[86] There is no law against reclining on the couch and eating chips yet.)

The new wisdom, the cutting edge of obesity studies, holds that there is no "ideal" weight, which Glenn Gaesser defines as "the weight at which the body feels healthy and is healthy."[87] This varies by individual, and forcing every single person on the planet into confinement in a little box on those absurd ideal height-weight charts is an exercise in physioterrorism. Let a thousand flowers bloom, let a thousand thighs and waistlines expand and contract. Excess weight itself is not the problem: it "may be nothing more than the visible, but benign, consequence of a sedentary lifestyle and poor dietary habits."[88] No one is saying that it's healthy to eat nothing but fats and sugar all day; but simply walking a walk to the post office; to work; hell to Dunkin' Donuts, for crying out loud, is far better for an obese person's health than dieting.

Physical activity is more important to one's health than macrobiotic diets and other forms of self-flagellation. "[I]n terms of health and longevity," says Stephen N. Blair, "your fitness level is far more important than your weight. If the heavy-weight charts say you are five pounds too heavy, or even fifty or more pounds too heavy, it is of little or no consequence healthwise *as long as you are physically fit*. On other hand, if you are a couch potato, being thin provides absolutely no assurance of good health, and does nothing to increase your chances of living a long life."[89]

Just how this new thinking regarding obesity affects the average fat person remains to be seen. Claudia Schiffer is not going to be replaced on the cover of *Cosmo* by Rosie O'Donnell. Men and women with sculpted bodies will still take pleasure in them, and even the most determined foe of the skinny police will grimace as he pinches a wattle of flab. Fat people are less likely to be married and more likely to be poor than thin people; that's probably not going to change. The diet industry may tighten its belt, but it's not going to dry up and disappear.

Yet perhaps a sensibleness can force its way into public discourse. It may take a while, but at some point the remark that Cornell University nutrition expert Dr. David Levitsky made to Laura Fraser may become the conventional wisdom: "Nobody ever dies of obesity. If you're a large person and you do not suffer from any other health problems, then there is no reason for you to lose weight."[90]

Who knows? Someday Americans may again take pleasure in eating, even in overeating. Chocolate does not kill; nor do spare ribs. The occasional barbecued potato chip, heck, the occasional bag of barbecued potato chips are not arsenic. Relax, America; eat up; *enjoy*. And take to heart, and stomach, the words of M.F.K. Fisher, doyenne of food writers, in her paean to the pleasures of occasional overindulgence:

> I cannot believe that there exists a single coherent human being who will not confess, at least to herself, that once or twice she had stuffed herself to the bursting point...for no other reason than the beastlike satisfaction of her belly. I pity anyone who has not permitted herself this sensual experience, if only to determine what her own private limitations are; and where, for herself alone, gourmandism ends and gluttony begins.[91]

3

Care for a Drink?

Forbidden fruit a flavor has
That lawful orchards mocks;
How luscious lies the pea within
The pod that Duty locks!
—Emily Dickinson

Though the "noble experiment" has been dead and buried for more than sixty years, there is still a Prohibition Party in America. Based in Denver, the party nominates a candidate for president every four years. The vote totals these days seldom exceed 20,000, however, a far cry from the 271,000 won by 1892 presidential candidate General John Bidwell, a Civil War veteran and reformed wine-maker who, on seeing the light, dug up his vines, donated his best vintage to San Francisco hospitals, and turned the rest of his grape into vinegar. The party still seeks to criminalize the manufacture and sale of alcohol, though its spokesmen insist, paradoxically, that Prohibitionists also desire "the end of excessive government regulation."[1] How do they fit the square peg into the round hole? By recasting prohibition as a health issue and not a political or philosophical matter. "It affects the public safety and welfare,"[2] says one former presidential candidate.

While the scattered band of party members may be gray and stooped, relics of a distant era, in this reformulation of an old tyranny as a new balm they are on the cutting edge.

Prohibition, even to many of those who lived through it from the ratification of the Eighteenth Amendment in 1919 through its repeal (by the Twenty-first Amendment) in 1933, seems like a strange dream. How did such a fantastic and improbable and primly repressive policy ever take hold? In the early 1920s, Charles Hanson Towne marveled, "The strange phenomenon of Prohibition...is still non-understandable to the majority of a great, and so-called free, people. It is one of the most astonishing manifestations the world has ever witnessed. It came upon us like a phantom, swiftly; like a thief in the night, taking us by surprise. Yet the prohibitionists will tell you that no one should be amazed, since for years—for almost a century—quiet forces have been at work to bring about this very thing."[3]

Those quiet forces, one must remember, did not call themselves prohibitionists. Even at its peak the Prohibition Party was nowhere near as potent as, say, the Socialist Party. The real power resided within such pressure groups as the Anti-Saloon League, whose very name was a triumph of nomenclature, in the tradition of Mothers Against Drunk Driving (what, are you *pro*-drunk driving?). To understand the modern busybodies, it is instructive to see how their predecessors operated.

Even the early Puritans, who always get a bad rap, were not prohibitionists. Drunkenness was a sin in their eyes, but they condoned moderate drinking. Temperance did not become a potent force in American life until the first half of the nineteenth century, when "a revolution in social attitudes took place: drinking ceased to be respectable,"[4] in the words of historian Ian R. Tyrrell. Temperance efforts led to a decline in per-capita alcohol consumption from more than five and one-half gallons in 1810 to four gallons in 1850; over that same period, per-capita consumption of distilled spirits fell from four and one-half to two and one-quarter gallons. This was significant, but as the figures reveal, Americans had hardly become teetotalers.

(It was at about this time that "teetotal" entered the language. In Lancashire, an English plasterer named Dickie Turner vowed never to get plastered again. A stutterer, Turner told a meeting, "I'll have nothing to do with this moderation, botheration pledge. I'll be right down tee-tee-total forever."[5])

The stateside Dickie Turners were also turning their backs on moderation. The American Temperance Society (ATS) was the first large organization dedicated to making America dry. The ATS was not a prohibitionist group; centered in New England, it counseled moral suasion to steer men from the bottle. When moral suasion failed, as it often does, more drastic though still private measures were called for: the ATS tried to convince Protestant denominations to excommunicate those who trafficked in, or in some cases simply consumed, alcoholic beverages. By 1833, the year of Dickie's rev-rev-revelation, there were more than 6,000 temperance societies in America, and perhaps one million persons had taken the pledge of "total abstinence." (There were many, many backsliders.)

From Moral Suasion to Law

But temperance advocates soon tired of moral suasion and began lobbying for laws restricting the sale and use of the demon rum. The voluntarist tools of the early temperance advocates—pledges, education, appeals to drunkards to consider the effects on their families—were no match for the long arm of the law. If you can't persuade 'em, the anti-alcohol crusaders soon learned, jail 'em.

In 1851 Maine enacted the first statewide prohibition law, the notorious Dow Act. Neal Dow, the law's namesake, was a Portland real-estate speculator and fanatical foe of spirits. His act was the "teeth" that law-and-order zealots are always demanding: it contained a "search-and-seizure" provision enabling state agents to barge into saloons and seize and destroy liquor. Dow's purer-than-puritan comrades rejoiced: deliverance from the great evil was at hand! Compulsory-education apostle Horace Mann exulted that the Maine law was equal to "the discovery of the magnetic needle, the invention of printing, or any other great strides in the progress of civilization."[6]

After Maine came the deluge: variants of prohibition came to Massachusetts, Minnesota, Rhode Island, and Vermont in 1852; Michigan in 1853; Connecticut in 1854; and New York, Indiana, Delaware, Iowa, Nebraska, and New Hampshire in 1855. But almost before you could say, "Do you have a warrant?" state courts were striking down the search-and-seizure provisions as violations of constitutional liberties. Public revulsion at the tyranny of prohibition was swift; within two decades, only three New England states remained dry.

But the pattern had been set. A moralistic crusade against drinking was followed by a series of increasingly repressive laws, culminating in blanket prohibition.

The Civil War played a mischievous part in nationalizing the prohibition movement. In 1862, Congress enacted the domestic liquors tax, which included a levy of one dollar per barrel on beer (and "within four months the United States Brewers' Association was formed"[7]). More importantly, the precedent for federal involvement in the heretofore local matter of alcohol regulation had been established. At the Constitutional Convention of 1787 a proposal to give Congress the power to make "sumptuary" laws had been overwhelmingly opposed; but here, in the crucible of war, a government desperate for tax money effectively rejected the Founders' wise counsel.

The next wave washed ashore in the 1870s. The newly formed Woman's Christian Temperance Union (WCTU) demonstrated that appeals to individual conscience were a thing of the past when it demanded:

> Resolved, That whereas, the object of just government is to conserve the best interests of the governed: and whereas the liquor traffic is not only a crime against God, but subversive of every interest of society; therefore, in behalf of humanity, we call for such legislation as shall secure this end: and while we will continue to employ all moral agencies as indispensable, we hold prohibition to be essential to the full triumph of this reform.[8]

In other words, sinner: Mend thy ways. For if thou doesn't, we'll throw you in jail. For your own good, of course.

The WCTU was positively temperate in tone when compared with the Anti-Saloon League (ASL). The League, which sat on the sturdy shoulders of Baptist, Methodist, Presbyterian, and Congregationalist members, traced its origin to an 1874 meeting in Oberlin, Ohio, which birthed the Oberlin Temperance Alliance. Oberlin was, and is, a college town, and the Oberlin Temperance Alliance, much like the neo-prohibitionists of MADD, demanded separation of college kid and bottle. The Alliance agitated for local option, that is, a popular vote to decide whether or not beer, wine, and liquor may be vended in college towns.

The Anti-Saloon League, which evolved from the Oberlin Temperance Alliance, was also pro-local option at first. Like all effective lobbies, the ASL threatened wet legislators with reprisal, and it had the might to back its threats up. The *American Issue*, the monthly organ of the Anti-Saloon League, had a circulation of over 500,000. (Among the financial angels of the ASL were A.I. Root, president of the Root Beer Company—now that's putting your money where your mouth is—and the Rockefeller family.)

The one-two punch packed by the WCTU and the ASL was enough to make Dean Martin sober. Even more sobering was the threat of one of Carry Nation's "hatchetations" the invasion of an army of ax-wielding saloon-busters. These folks were not the sort to give serious consideration to opposing points of view. As the Kentucky edition of the *American Issue* editorialized:

> The saloon is the storm center of crime; the devil's headquarters on earth; the school-master of a broken decalogue; the defiler of youth; the enemy of the home;

the foe of peace; the deceiver of nations; the beast of sensuality; the past master of intrigue; the vagabond of poverty; the social vulture; the rendezvous of demagogues; the enlisting office of sin; the serpent of Eden; a ponderous second edition of hell, revised, enlarged and illuminated.[9]

Remember that the next time you stop off for a beer.

Indoctrinate the Children...

"Our children are in danger while the saloon stands,"[10] warned the Anti-Saloon League. Like contemporary nanny groups, the prohibitionists lobbied politicians while propagandizing amongst the young. The ASL distributed material on "scientific temperance" to public and Sunday schools; the League's torrential output included plays, songs, scripts for recital, and such poems as "The Price of an Ohio License":

What's the price of a license? How much did you say?
The price of men's souls in the market today?
A license to sell, to deform, to destroy,
From the gray hairs of age to the innocent boy.
How much did you say?[11]

No rhyme was too hackneyed for the *American Issue*. And the leitmotif was usually children:

Women and Children First, 'tis the law of the sea,
But why not make it the rule wherever a man may be?
Let it become the law where roisterers quench their thirst,
Emblazon it over the bar 'Women and Children First.'[12]

The WCTU's Department of Scientific Temperance Instruction bullied legislatures in every state and territory into mandating temperance education in the public schools. The WCTU set up a panel to give its imprimatur to school texts; it demanded that texts teach that "alcohol is a dangerous and seductive poison."[13] By 1906 this panel, which had pledged itself to "a prolonged struggle...to free our public-school system from the incubus which rests upon it," had endorsed 40 texts for classroom use. The WCTU's Mrs. Mary Hannah Hunt saw the blessed day of deliverance "surely coming when from the school houses all over the land will come trained haters of alcohol to pour a whole Niagara of ballots upon the saloon."[14]

And what did these pint-sized haters imbibe in their classrooms? The ASL taught that insanity, tuberculosis, and epilepsy were linked to alcohol. It alleged that "10 percent of the deaths, annually, in the United

States are due to alcohol."[15] The WCTU's Department of Scientific Temperance Instruction taught the following as incontrovertible facts:

1. The majority of beer drinkers die from dropsy.
2. When [alcohol] passes down the throat it burns off the skin leaving it bare and burning.
3. It causes the heart to beat many unnecessary times, and after the first dose the heart is in danger of giving out so that it needs something to keep it up and, therefore, the person to whom the heart belongs has to take drink after drink to keep his heart going.
4. It turns the blood to water.
5. A[n invalid] man who never drinks liquor will get well, where a drinking man would surely die.[16]

Of course, this is sheer nonsense to modern ears, although before we get too smug we might wonder how the pronouncements of our own Drug Warriors will strike American sensibilities in the year 2098. At all events, the propaganda campaign in the schools was a smashing success. No less a personage than the U.S. Commissioner of Education said in 1920: "In the creation of a sentiment which has resulted first in local option, then in state prohibition, and now in national prohibition, the schools of the country have played a very important part; in fact probably a major part.... The instruction in physiology and hygiene with special reference to the effects of alcohol...has resulted first in clear thinking, and second in better and stronger sentiment in regard to the sale of alcoholic drinks."[17]

The goal, as prohibitionists then and now believed, was to indoctrinate the children while they're young and impressionable. The "Just Say No" campaign of the war on drugs was aimed at schoolkids, as was one of its bizarre offshoots, the effort to induce children to turn their pot-smoking parents in to the authorities. (This horrifying scheme, which peaked in 1985, has since been de-emphasized, though chilling Orwellian echoes remain.) The modern-day MADD and its student branch, SADD, are, ostensibly, vehicles for dissuading teenagers from drinking and driving—a praiseworthy aim. But as we shall see, MADD has increasingly ventured into WCTU territory: it is neo-prohibitionist, while always carefully disclaiming the prohibitionist label.

The mass media, as is the case today, eagerly cooperated in the campaign for prohibition. The editor of *McClure's* wrote hogwash of this sort: "Every function of the normal human body is injured by the use of alcohol even the moderate use; and that injury is both serious and permanent."[18]

To those who objected that prohibition violated personal liberties, the editor of the popular monthly the *Gospel of the Kingdom* retorted: "'Personal liberty' is at last an uncrowned, dethroned King, with no one to do him reverence. The social consciousness is so far developed, and is becoming so autocratic, that institutions and governments must give their heed to its mandate and shape their life accordingly. We are no longer frightened by that ancient bogy 'paternalism in government.' We affirm boldly, it is the business of government to be just that paternal."[19]

At least this is honest: an unashamed, unequivocating endorsement of tyranny. There is none of the CSPI-ish dissimulation. The *Gospel of the Kingdom* was pro-Goliath, without apologies; the first order of business in their brave new world, one can be sure, would be the outlawing of slingshots.

Others were cannier. A chief strategist of the Anti-Saloon League advised members to avoid getting dragged into arguments about such sacred doctrines as "Personal Liberty," the "Sanctity of the Home," "Home Rule," and "States' Rights." Instead, he suggested, make sure the discussion displays "liquor always in its sordid nakedness of drugging and destroying humanity for filthy lucre."[20]

Just as our modern liquor-loathers indict potables for every little economic slump (how can a nation of beer drinkers compete with the Japanese, for goodness sake?) so did their forbears. The *Manufacturer's Record* editorialized: "Drastic prohibition would increase the efficiency of the army. It would increase the efficiency of the workers in industrial plants and mining operations. It would increase the efficiency of men on the farms and add enormously to the potential power of the nation."[21] As for those sluggards who didn't want to shape up and make good soldiers or peons, one prohibitionist had a final solution for them: "It would be a saving to the Nation if we could kill off all its hard drinkers tomorrow. There are two and one-half million of these, and their first cost, at twenty-one years of age, was at least *five billions of dollars*."[22] (While it is outside the scope of this book, note that cigarette smokers nowadays are faulted in much the same terms: as drains on our treasury and economy.)

...And Practice Not-So-Subtle Racism

Racism was never far from the surface of the prohibition movement. Will Irwin in *Collier's Weekly* spoke for his generation of racists in 1908:

The primitive Negro field hand, a web of strong, sudden impulses, good and bad, comes into town or settlement on Saturday afternoon and pays his fifty cents for a pint of Mr. Levy's gin. He absorbs not only its toxic heat, but absorbs also the suggestion, subtly conveyed, that it contains aphrodisiacs. He sits in the road or in the alley at the height of his debauch, looking at that obscene picture of a white woman on the label, drinking in the invitation which it carries. And then comes opportunity. There follows the hideous episode of the rope or the stake."[23]

The bottle, in the feverish minds of Irwin and his fellow racists, gave us interracial rape and the lynch mob. The solution was to keep alcohol out of the hands and mouths of irresponsible childlike Negroes. They were simply incapable of exercising good judgment when booze was nearby.

Thank goodness such attitudes have been banished from the good ole USA. Or have they? The premise of the Center for Science in the Public Interest's book, *Marketing Booze to Blacks* (1987), is that child-like blacks are so beguiled, so hypnotized by liquor ads that they just can't help themselves. For its patronizing tone and racist assumptions, *Marketing Booze to Blacks* may as well have been written in dialect: "Looky heah at that faaahn blond on de Black Velvet billboard—let's git drunk and rape white women!"

The book's publication was subsidized, in part, by those friends of the black working man at the Rockefeller Family Fund. As with *Marketing Disease to Hispanics*, *Marketing Booze to Blacks* features a preface by a licensed minority person, in this case the late, respected Congresswoman Barbara Jordan (D-Tex.), who calls for "a full-scale, frontal assault on alcohol, as one of the many drugs that is undermining our community."[24] It is not clear what she means by "full-scale, frontal assault," but her lumping beer with other "drugs" suggests that the law ought to treat it as such, but then, CSPI is always savvy enough not to mention the P-word in its publications.

Marketing Booze to Blacks is classic CSPI. It opens with the breathless assertion that "beer, wine, and liquor producers aggressively seek to maximize sales of their products."[25] Horrors! Just think: businessmen actively trying to sell their wares; what atrocities will they commit next? Particularly noxious is the practice of the alcohol industry in advertising in black-oriented magazines, on black-oriented radio, and using advertising agencies run by blacks. The use of black celebrities and models in advertisements is condemned; so is the unconscionable sponsorship by alcohol companies of events related to Black History Month.

In uncharacteristically dry language, the CSPI authors allege that "alcohol abuse's links to physical violence have been extreme for black

Americans, particularly males."[26] Murders, assaults, general hooligan-ism: it seems that black men and booze just don't mix. Of course, this is exactly what Will Irwin was talking about in *Collier's*; the "primitive Negro field hand" could no more hold his liquor than the black man on the street corner in the CSPI book.

The black-owned advertising agencies in Chicago, New York, and elsewhere that handle accounts for such companies as Jack Daniels, Seagram, and Miller Brewing target "the most popular types of music, sports, and cultural events enjoyed by blacks,"[27] fret the authors. Now you might think that this is a fine example of black capitalism, but you would be wrong. This is the most devious form of exploitation! Black agencies selling products that black consumers enjoy: don't they know that nigras can't hold their booze?

Alcoholic beverages that are pitched primarily to blacks, for instance Heileman's Colt-45 malt liquor whose consumers are about three-fourths black, get a special place in the CSPI hell. You see, malt liquors like Colt-45 and King Cobra typically contain more alcohol by volume than beer, and you know what alcohol does to those people.

Black-oriented magazines such as *Ebony* and *JET* are condemned for selling ad space to liquor companies as though the Rockefeller money that CSPI takes is as pure as the driven snow. And yet these magazines, products as they are of the nasty profit system, refuse to carry "public-service" (that is, nonpaying, freeloading) ads that tell readers not to buy the products advertised on the previous page. Besides, "alcohol marketers tell black consumers that drinking is the ticket to success and prosperity."[28] Apparently, childlike black consumers will not fig-ure out that a glass of cognac does not magically make five million dollars appear in your bank account; they need great white fathers like CSPI's Michael Jacobson to set them straight.

Any advertisement featuring black sexuality sends Jacobson into a tizzy. Print ads for Seagram's Gin that "depict a black couple in a pas-sionate embrace shirt open, hands roaming"[29] ought to be outlawed, he suggests.

CSPI scorns billboards as a truly loathsome advertising vehicle. An ad for Lord Calvert Canadian whisky featuring Wilt Chamberlain and the slogan "Up Where You Belong" is not a reference to Wilt's seven-foot stature but "a not so subtle message...that one deserves to be high."[30]

The message throughout *Marketing Booze to Blacks* is loud and clear: don't. For "alcohol promotions to blacks (and certain other minority groups) require special attention, because large numbers of blacks are particularly vulnerable to alcohol problems due to their unique health, economic, and social status."[31] By "special attention" the authors mean federal regulation; yes, the federal government should prevent companies in this erstwhile land of the free from advertising to black people who CSPI would have us believe are too feebleminded to resist its siren song. First Amendment, Thirst Amendment.

The most telling part of any CSPI publication is the list of solutions at the end, and *Marketing Booze to Blacks* is no exception. It proposes a whole range of statist measures, from steep increases in excise taxes to advertising bans to more federal programs to unspecified "effective means of preventing and reducing drinking problems."[32] (These "effective means" always seem to involve the policeman's nightclub, the judge's sentence, and the jailer's key.) Uncle Sam should step in and "set a maximum alcohol content for malt beverages of 5 percent by volume,"[33] because, after all, those people just can't...well, you get the idea. The offensive racist assumptions of the nanny statists simply haven't changed over the years.

We've Got to Do Something about "Those People"

But back to those earlier prohibitionists. Concerned as they were about blacks, they also found time to malign the working-class and immigrants. In 1908 the Maryland edition of the *American Issue* responded to a German-American group's ringing endorsement of freedom of choice: "Really, is not the country growing rather tired of having a lot of swill-fattened, blowsy half-foreigners getting together and between hiccoughs laying down definitions to Americans regarding the motive of our constitution and laws?"[34]

The motives of those who defended liberty were often impugned. The Ohio edition of the *American Issue* remarked: "Occasionally some poor specimen of humanity, leaning over a saloon bar and looking through the bottom of a beer glass, condemns the Anti-Saloon League for its activity in politics.... Of course the Anti-Saloon League is in politics.... It is in politics to keep the brewers and liquor dealers from filling offices with their tools and from hanging a beer sign above the doors of legislative halls."[35]

As the incomparable H.L. Mencken described it: "The Prohibitionist leaders, being mainly men of wide experience in playing upon the prejudices and emotions of the mob, developed a technique of terrorization that was almost irresistible. The moment a politician ventured to speak against them he was accused of the grossest baseness. It was whispered that he was a secret drunkard and eager to safeguard his tipple; it was covertly hinted that he was in the pay of the Whiskey Ring, the Beer Trust, or some other such bugaboo. The events showed that the shoe was actually on the other foot—that many of the principal supporters of Prohibition were on the payroll of the Anti-Saloon League, and that judges, attorneys general, and other high officers of justice afterward joined them there. But the accusations served their purpose."[36]

"If we wish to purify politics, the saloon must be destroyed,"[37] one League speaker declared, and this has been the chilling theme of totalitarian utopians everywhere: if we can just root out and destroy the evildoers, then we will have created an Eden on earth. No matter that the cost is always measured in lost liberties and, all too often, innocent lives. All hail the vision of perfected humanity perfected by deploying the instrument of the state like a hatchet. As the baseball-playing evangelist Billy Sunday imagined, prohibition would bring about a world in which "the slums will soon be only a memory. We will turn our prisons into factories and our jails into storehouses and corncribs. Men will walk upright now, women will smile and the children will laugh. Hell will be forever for rent."[38]

Prohibition was a crashing failure. So much so that it all but eliminated the P-word from political discourse. Upon its repeal in 1933, men and women confidently asserted that never again would a band of crazed fanatical puritans dare take on the American's cherished right to drink.

Historian Jack S. Blocker, Jr., has speculated that had the temperance crusaders stuck to their strategy of local option and moral suasion and not listened to the siren's song of the Eighteenth Amendment, "America would today have a healthy prohibition movement instead of senile, isolated temperance groups."[39] But he spoke too soon. Since Blocker wrote in 1976, America has seen the return of the prohibitionists, though today they bear such names as Mothers Against Drunk Driving and the Center for Science in the Public Interest.

The more things change, the more nanny remains the same. Just as the WCTU and ASL rose from the ashes of the antebellum Dow Act, so have MADD and her ilk emerged from the swamp of the Eighteenth Amendment.

"We're now picking up a thread which got dropped with the fuss that went on around Prohibition,"[40] said Robin Room, director of the federally subsidized Alcohol Research Center in Berkeley, California.

Room made his observation in the *New York Times* in 1985; James Kirby Martin, a professor of history at the University of Houston, concurred: "It's pretty clear to me that we have entered a kind of neo-temperance, neo-Prohibitionist phase of activity in the United States.... I think we're in a long-term anti-alcohol cycle."[41]

Nanny Gets MADD

This time, the prohibitionists have an even better name. Only the most insensitive, hardened brute could raise even the mildest objection to an organization whose public face is that of grieving mothers whose children were killed by drunk drivers. Of course driving while intoxicated is and should be a crime, and the grief and bereavement that devastates those who lose a loved one to such a senseless act is immeasurable. And yet...and yet....

The agenda of Mothers Against Drunk Driving is the most insidious kind of neo-prohibitionism, cloaked in the unassailable garb of family loss. MADD was founded by a California woman named Candy Lightner after her thirteen-year-old daughter, Cari, was killed in 1980 by a drunk driver as the girl was walking to a school carnival.

MADD is no longer a mom-and-pop operation. It has swollen into a huge nonprofit bureaucracy, with a budget of approximately $50 million, a staff approaching 300 persons, and 400 chapters worldwide. It is credited with three million "members and supporters," but groups routinely lie about membership, often claiming names on a mailing list as "members" or "supporters," so the truth, while it is out there, is somewhat murky.

Theoretically, MADD, as a nonprofit organization, is forbidden from lobbying, but then, theoretically, the authors could also be the opposing quarterbacks in next year's Super Bowl. In practice, this stricture is a joke, observed mainly in the breach. MADD members, along with the insurance industry and the secretary of transportation, were the prime movers in the 1984 decree from Washington that states raise their drinking ages to twenty-one. (For details, see chapter 4.)

But MADD is not necessarily what its name suggests. First, the membership is *not* primarily composed of bereft mothers; MADD director Robert L. Beck estimates that perhaps 40 percent of its members have lost someone in a drunk-driving accident.[42] The rest are "interested citizens," says Mr. Beck, which can either be read "interested citizens" or "busybodies who like to stick their noses into other peoples' business."

MADD has been embroiled in internecine conflict and has drawn sharp outside criticism. In 1985 its executive committee stripped President Candy Lightner of her additional titles of chairman and chief executive officer after the group had been blasted by the Council of Better Business Bureaus and the National Charities Information Bureau for "spending too little on its programs and too much on fund-raising efforts,"[43] according to the *New York Times*.

The *NonProfit Times*, a trade publication, condemned MADD as one of the nonprofits that spends the most on fund raising and the least on actual programs. In 1990, "the group's telephone campaign collected $35 million. Some seventy-two cents of each dollar went to the people behind the campaign not toward fighting drunken driving."[44]

MADD has raised the eyebrows of other nanny groups by sometimes lying down with the devil. Cindi Lamb, a co-founder of the organization whose seven-year-old daughter was killed by a drunk driver, was a paid consultant to the National Beer Wholesalers Association. The alcohol industry-funded Century Council has cooperated with MADD in programs to encourage "moderate drinking." A junior group, Students Against Drunk Driving (SADD), founded by former high-school teacher and hockey coach Robert Anastas and now active in more than 25,000 high schools, junior highs, and colleges, was subsidized in part by Anheuser-Busch until 1988.

"If they're not sincere," Anastas said of the brewers, distillers, and winemakers who pump as much as $100 million annually into the temperance movement, "there's going to be the biggest backlash against the alcohol industry.... But you have to give people a break. If the alcohol industry has 'sinned,' then let them clean up their act!"[45] In the Middle Ages they called this practice simony, or the selling of church pardons. It is not exactly clear what "sins" the alcohol manufacturers have committed since when is manufacturing and selling one of the world's oldest refreshments sinful? But just cough up a few million, Anheuser-Busch, and your critics will turn down the volume a notch or two. If the word "blackmail" comes to mind, well, you said it, we didn't.

Andrew McGuire, an original MADD director, has criticized this sort of relationship, asking, "Would you want the Mafia underwriting anti-crime programs?"[46] A nice line, though it reveals something of the MADD mentality: these people regard drinking itself—not drinking and driving—as criminal, and if they ever have their way the Noble Experiment will get an encore, this time with beefed-up enforcement and a modern media propaganda barrage.

Yet another neo-prohibitionist pressure group, this one based in up-state New York, goes by the acronym RID, for Remove Intoxicated Drivers (from what, one wonders?; their automobiles? polite society? this planet?). But lest the reader get the impression that the anti-alcohol campaign is made up of energetic private organizations that, however wrong-headed, are at least genuinely grass roots, we hasten to identify the thumbprints of the federal government.

Located in the bowels of the mammoth Department of Health and Human Services, created in 1986 during the Reagan-era rebirth of American prohibitionism, it goes by the ungainly name of the Center (formerly Office) for Substance Abuse Prevention (CSAP). Its budget, which usually works out to somewhere between $250 and $300 million annually, is spent printing and disseminating reams of anti-drug and anti-booze propaganda, sponsoring conferences of busybodies, and creating and distributing films about "substance abuse" that have all the depth and honesty of a typical 1934 Soviet cinema production about a boy and his tractor.

This kind of agitprop is not a legitimate function of Washington in the first place, but even if you think it is, CSAP and its grantees are forbidden by law to use government monies for "publicity or propaganda purposes, for the preparation, distribution, or use of any kit, pamphlet, booklet, publication, radio, television, or film presentation designed to support or defeat legislation pending before the Congress."[47]

CSAP has consistently violated the law by publishing propaganda and sponsoring conferences that encourage lobbying for the passage of bills on the puritan agenda. In 1993, the U.S. General Accounting Office slapped its bureaucratic wrist for these violations, though it is what GAO *did not* condemn that is the real crime. Among CSAP's activities:

- It has promoted "Artfux" (don't sound it out), an otherwise unemployable band of annoying people who deface billboards that advertise alcohol.[48]
- It funded a video intended as a how-to for "activists" in other states about a California campaign to raise excise taxes on alcohol. This did not violate the law, GAO found, because the restrictions on lobbying apply only to federal legislation. In other words, Washington can fund lobbying at the state level, a rather extraordinary advance in governmental relations.[49]
- It sponsored a publication that demanded enactment of a virtual nanny utopia: an increase in the federal tax on beer of 455 percent; the reduction of the legal definition of drunkenness from the typical blood alcohol content level of .10 to .04; and the requirement that beer ads be countered by anti-beer ads, to be paid for by you-know-who.[50]

David Rehr of the National Beer Wholesalers Association says, "It drives our wholesalers nuts to know that their tax dollars are being used by groups that are trying to drive them out of business."[51] As it should.

The language that CSAP grantees use and cannot use, according to CSAP guidelines, reeks of totalitarianism. Its *Policy Review Guidelines* and *Communications Review Guidelines* declare, "Materials recommending a designated driver should be rated unacceptable."[52] Designated drivers imply that *someone* might drink, you see, and that's a no-no. In the CSAP future of a .04 BAC, a 140-pounder who downs two beers will be drunk; we will *all* be designated drivers then. Publications that acknowledge "moderate" drinking are also unacceptable.

Professor Raymond P. Lorion, who contributed to a CSAP monograph, argued for "the creation of an environment in which substance use, regardless of the form it takes, is defined clearly and consistently as unacceptable."[53]

Note the use of "use." Not "abuse," mind you, but "use." One beer, one glass of wine, one cocktail: clearly and consistently unacceptable. However much they protest, these people fattened on government grants are prohibitionists.

Again, we cannot repeat enough: drunk driving is and should be a crime, and those who injure or kill another person while driving a vehicle under the influence of alcohol should be punished to the fullest measure of the law. To the extent that MADD and SADD and RID promote meliorist measures such as "designated drivers" and free taxi service for drunkards and encourage young people to think twice before mixing cars and booze, then more power to them. SADD's "Contract for Life" in which young people pledge to call their parents for a ride if ever they or their drivers have been drinking, and parents agree to pick them up, no questions asked, is a fine idea. Among MADD's better programs is a face-to-face encounter session described by Jane Lewis Engelke, president of the Eastern Connecticut Mothers Against Drunk Driving:

> But since laws alone cannot change public attitudes, I and other members of MADD often speak in schools, before civic groups and senior citizens organizations. In a new effort to reduce recidivism, victims including those who have lost children, spouses, and siblings are addressing offenders in a nonaccusatory manner, telling the stories of what drunk driving has done to their lives. This helps offenders to understand better the enormous consequences of a crime which often involves a stranger and is frequently not remembered."[54]

A worthy program. And the heart-wrenching testimony of the bereaved ought to sear into the memories of those on the receiving end a simple and timeless message: Do Not Drive While Drunk.

But, alas, Mrs. Engelke's first clause "since laws alone cannot change public attitudes" reveals MADD's troubling flaw. Laws alone may not be able to change public attitudes, so they say, but they're a good start. "Laws make morals," went a chilling adage of the early twentieth-century totalitarians, and if we have learned anything over the course of this sometimes very bloody century it is to have no truck with those who would use the law—the police, the courts, the military, the state—to enforce their notions of proper private behavior on the rest of us.

The MADD agenda "education," which somehow ceases to be tutorial and slowly elides into a series of government restrictions, is simply an updated version of the program of the Woman's Christian Temperance Union (WCTU).

Not that the WCTU itself hasn't tried to adapt to the times. It is hard to imagine refashioning the pious lady prohibitionists of the 1870s as minivan-driving soccer moms, but, incredibly, there is still a WCTU. It claims 150,000 members in the United States, though pressure groups have been known to exaggerate such numbers in the past. Even so, it is almost certainly bigger than the current Prohibition Party.

The new WCTU "Not Your Mother's Woman's Christian Temperance Union," as the image consultant's slogan might go sounds an awful lot like.... well, Mothers Against Drunk Driving. Five hundred members met in Beckley, West Virginia, in August 1990 to kick off the WCTU's campaign for the 1990s. President Rachel Kelly explained their mission: "We believe in teaching children not to start drinking. Then someday we'll be able to sit back and watch legalized prohibition."[55] Note the way Ms. Kelly seamlessly joins the seemingly innocuous concept of education to the Big Brother decree of prohibition.

Spokesman (yes, men may join as honorary members) Michael Vitucci explains, "These are very intelligent women who realize that the alcohol industry has a great stranglehold on this nation. The WCTU belies that today with education...our youth will hopefully place a self-prohibition on these substances."[56]

Again, note the linkage of "education" and the P-word, though Vitucci is savvy enough to add the prefix "self."

By an instructive coincidence, the surging of MADD was simultaneous with a harshly repressive and counterproductive crackdown on drinking in what was then still the Soviet Union.

Russians have never much gone for tee-tee-total temperance. The new communist government tried to enforce a blanket prohibition in the early 1920s, just as their supposedly opposite numbers did stateside, and it met with a predictable lack of success. There are some habits that even the gulag can't break. As Professor Nis-Adolph Petersen of Jersey State College explained, "When Vladimir, Grand Duke of Kievan Russia, sought a new religion for his pagan subjects, he was at first attracted to Islam. It offered a number of advantages—but one aspect, its prohibition of alcohol, caused Vladimir to reject it. 'To drink,' Vladimir reputedly said, 'is the joy of the Russ!' He was consequently baptized in the Christian faith in 988 and ordered his people converted as well, thus making Russia part of the Western rather than the Islamic world."[57]

So when Mikhail Gorbachev initiated stringent liquor laws in 1985, he was battling not only a nation besotted by seventy years of communistic stupor but a proud (if occasionally staggering) tradition of nearly 1,000 years. The millennium of Russian Christianity came, and went, and so did Mikhail Gorbachev, replaced by Boris Yeltsin, a man whose appetite for hard liquor made Grand Duke Vladimir look like a Sunday school teacher.

The Gorbachev crackdown took a cue from the United States. Indeed, the parallels are sometimes remarkable. The Soviets instituted police roadblocks and random sobriety checks for drivers, as were the rage on American roads. Liquor store hours were squeezed into just five hours in the afternoon and early evening, which did not so much discourage consumption as it did beget absenteeism.

Alcohol production was slashed, so drunks switched to eau de cologne or industrial solvent which, unlike vodka, can kill the imbiber on the spot. As *Izvestia* noted, "From port and vodka, the die-hard alcoholics have been shifting to perfumes and industrial fluids containing spirits. Doctors are becoming alarmed. The number of cases of poisoning has risen sharply."[58] (Rubber cement cut with salt was a favorite of Russia's less discriminating topers: As one young man who once drank a glass of this in Siberia explained to the *Los Angeles Times*, "I thought I was going to die. It completely paralyzed my face, and I literally couldn't speak for twenty minutes."[59]

As state liquor stores closed, a vigorous black market appeared, with old women in shawls selling streetcorner elixirs. The drinking age was raised from eighteen to twenty-one, as Gorby did his best Ronald Reagan impersonation. Adults who supplied intoxicants to children—even a parent giving wine to a child—was at risk of punishment ranging from imprisonment to what was so charmingly known as "corrective labor." Home brewers were arrested, in best J. Edgar Hoover versus the moonshiners style. As the black market prospered, government revenues fell; liquor taxes had once supplied one-eighth of Moscow's revenues.

The Soviet campaign included a propaganda element not unlike the MADD agenda. Beginning at age seven, schoolchildren were subjected to anti-alcohol indoctrination. Television commercials emphasized such unnatural practices as booze-less weddings. Movies were edited to remove scenes of festive drinking, much as Hollywood was pressured to snip at films that displayed cigarette or drug usage as casual and enjoyable activities.

Though ordinary Russians chafed at the restrictions, the about-to-disintegrate Communist Party huzzahed. "The abuse of alcohol is so far quite often not regarded as an immoral, antisocial conduct," declared the party's Central Committee. "The force of the law and of public opinion is not applied to drunkards in full volume."[60] Allowing for the awkwardness of the translation, is that really any different from what MADD has been saying for its almost two decades of existence?

After a year of anti-alcohol zealotry, even the most fervent communists admitted that things had gone too far. "Administrative over-zealousness is overcoming good sense,"[61] editorialized *Pravda*, in response to reader complaints that passengers on city buses had been given breath-analyses. ("Why didn't *we* think of that?" one imagines a WCTU worker sighing.) Even *Pravda* urged the prohibitionists to have "a respectful attitude toward people, barring infringement of citizens' rights and dignity."[62] Would that our own media, which cooperated with the mid-1980s clampdown on alcohol consumption, had evinced a *Pravda*-like concern for the rights of those individuals who chose to drink responsibly.

But despite the labors of the neo-prohibitionists, the taste for strong drink seems almost innate; our thirsts will not be slaked by near-beer. Dr. Barbara S. McCrady, a psychologist and professor at Rutgers Center for Alcohol Studies, worried in 1985 that the temperance boom would be short-lived. "The cynical side of me says we'll have another swing of the pendulum in another twenty years, when people will reject all this external control."[63]

Well, one can only hope, and there are hopeful signs. The martini has made a comeback; health nannys are parodied regularly on the wittier television comedies, and a growing percentage of Americans tell pollsters they don't trust their government to do the right thing. And why, oh why, should they?

4

None for the Road

*Our country has deliberately undertaken a
great social and economic experiment noble in
spirit and far reaching in purpose.*
—Herbert Hoover (1928)

Ever since the Oberlin Temperance Association campaigned to make
college towns dry, young adults have been the subject of nanny's so-
licitude. So it is no surprise that the neo-prohibitionists scored their
greatest recent success in 1984, when President Ronald Reagan, at the
urging of his transportation secretary, Elizabeth Dole, signed into law a
measure that withheld federal highway monies from those states that
did not raise their drinking ages to twenty-one.

This was no mere nuisance: states that did not follow Washington's
orders would lose 5 percent of their federal highway money the first
year and an additional 10 percent every year thereafter, meaning that
by the mid-1990s states that had funny notions about their rights would
be getting exactly nothing back from a highway trust fund made fat by
taxes on their motorists and truckers. (Attaching strings to federal dis-
bursements is a wonderfully indirect way to bend states to Uncle Sam's
will; almost one-third of all dollars spent by state and local governments are from federal grants-in-aid.)

Mind you, there was no solid evidence that this thunderbolt from
Mount Washington would have any effect whatsoever on the rate of
traffic fatalities. That didn't matter. What counted was that this decree
provided politicians with a cheap chance to come out strongly in favor
of...Life! Those harmed by the measure besides the fifty states, which
had previously been thought to have the power to set their own drinking ages were eighteen-, nineteen-, and twenty-year-old kids: not coin-
cidentally, the adult cohort who votes least. The Senate passed the

twenty-one bill by a landslide, 81–16; the House did not even bother to poll the individual members, passing the bill by voice vote. Compare the ease with which millions of Americans were deprived of an erstwhile right with the glacial pace of a state-level reform that might actually make a difference: requiring elderly motorists to retake drivers' license tests every couple of years. But then the American Association of Retired Persons means business, and last we checked there was no American Association of Young Adults.

Wait, you say: didn't President Reagan profess a belief in the federalist system, under which states are no mere appendages of the federal Leviathan but sovereign entities capable of deciding such matters within their own legislatures, without the interfering hand of Congress? Well, he said so now and then. So did Mrs. Dole. "In all my efforts to promote safer transportation," she wrote later, "I tried to respect individual choice."[1] But as we have seen time and again, there are always *special circumstances* that require that individual choice be set aside and the preferences of the nanny state be imposed.

Ironically, in his listless campaign for the presidency in 1996, Secretary Dole's husband took to pulling a copy of the Tenth Amendment from his pocket and waving it at the crowd, promising to give new life to this forgotten amendment, which reads, in its entirety, "The powers not delegated to the United States by the Constitution, nor prohibited by it to the states, are reserved to the States respectively, or to the people." As there is no obvious constitutional grant to the federal government to regulate drinking ages within the states, one might have thought that Bob Dole would, in his first hour as president, call for the repeal of Secretary Dole's edict. But no. To Bob Dole, and most of his colleagues, states' rights cease when the states exercise them in the wrong way. Bob Dole waving a copy of the Tenth Amendment was about as convincing as Teddy Kennedy brandishing a copy of the Sixth Commandment.

Neo-prohibitionist Christine Lubinksi of the National Council on Alcoholism, asked by *Reason* magazine to defend this usurpation of states' rights, replied, "The evidence was overwhelming that an increase in the drinking age led to a reduction in drunk-driving fatalities." (This is untrue, by the way, but we'll let it slide for now.) "I don't give a damn, frankly, about whether [the law] was appropriate."[2] And that's that. Like Rhett Butler, these people don't give a damn—not about Scarlett O'Hara, but about the rather more fragile U.S. Constitution.

Fighting the Feds

Not every state buckled under to the 1984 law. But, alas, money usually trumps principles. New York was among the first to cave in, the spokesman for Governor Mario Cuomo insisting that "saving lives was the main reason the Governor pushed for this measure."[3] Others held out against what South Dakota Governor George Mickelson called "blackmail."[4]

The honor role of resisters included Wyoming, Colorado, Idaho, Montana, and South Dakota. These states held out longest against the Dole-Reagan edict, but even they were eventually brought low: the highways have to be maintained, after all. (South Dakota and Colorado were not exactly paradise for under-twenty-ones in search of rollicking fun: the states permitted nineteen- and twenty-year olds to drink only low-alcohol 3.2 beer.)

"After a while, you just get tired of somebody else telling you what to do," complained Wyoming State Representative Hardy Tate. "The fact that somebody can come in and willy-nilly pick a group of people and deprive them of their privileges is beyond anything I would ever do. Besides, I fully believe nineteen-year olds are adults."[5]

Doughty South Dakota, joined by Wyoming and Idaho, brought suit against the federal government, contending that the law violated the Twenty-first Amendment, which had in 1933 repealed the prohibitionist Eighteenth Amendment and restored to the states the right to make laws regarding "the transportation or importation…of intoxicating liquors."

This would seem fairly cut and dried, but of course it was not. The Department of Justice, in its brief, asserted that the drinking-age law did not "coerce" the fifty states into bringing their respective drinking ages up to twenty-one; no, it merely offered a financial "incentive." This incentive was justified by "the Federal Government's substantial interest in promoting safety on the Nation's highways and the health of the nation's teenage youth."[6] Once it is established that the "health of the nation's teenage youth" is a justification for ignoring the Constitution, there is precious little that Washington cannot do.

In any event, the Supreme Court found the Justice Department's argument compelling, and today all fifty of our states prohibit young men and women who are old enough to die in wars and enter into legal contracts from buying a beer at a local tavern. Or at least theoretically they are prohibited from doing so, for as the South Dakota Attorney

General, Mark V. Meierhenry, argued before the Court in *South Dakota v. Dole*, no. 86-260, the old laws permitted "legal drinking, as opposed to the surreptitious drinking that will inevitably occur"[7] and which has, inevitably, occurred.

For just seven years after Congress and President Reagan foisted the twenty-one-year-old drinking age on us, three-quarters of those surveyed thought that teen drinking had become an even bigger problem than in the carefree days of every state for itself. And it had.

"The law sets off a psychology of forbidden fruit among young people that gives alcohol an attractiveness it doesn't deserve,"[8] charges Dr. Morris Chafetz, the founding director of the National Institute of Alcohol Abuse and Alcoholism. Tom Goodale, vice president for student affairs at Virginia Tech, agrees. "You could throw all of the resources in the world into enforcement, but you're missing the point. By making drinking illegal under the age of twenty-one, we have glorified the ritual, put it on a pedestal."[9] This is exactly what happened, on a broader scale, during Prohibition. As economic historian Mark Thornton has written, "It heightened the attractiveness of alcohol to the young by making it a glamour product associated with excitement and intrigue."[10] Even today, one survey found that Utah, Kentucky, and Mississippi, which have some of the most restrictive alcohol laws in the country, also have the most severe problems with alcoholism.

The "forbidden fruit" argument was seconded by Professor Thomas Pettigrew, a University of California-Santa Cruz social scientist: "There is a lot of evidence to show that people react negatively when a freedom, an option that was there, is removed, even if that option wasn't very important to them. I'm told by older people that liquor never tasted better than during prohibition."[11]

Or as a nineteen-year-old boy on Long Island told the *New York Times* on the eve of the increased drinking age: "It will be neat, like sneaking a cigarette behind the house when you're a kid."[12]

Public-health scientist Elizabeth M. Whelan, president of the American Council on Science and Health and mother of an "underage" daughter, writes that from her "observations of Christine and her friends' predicament about drinking, I believe that today's laws are unrealistic. Prohibiting the sale of liquor to responsible young adults creates an atmosphere where binge drinking and alcohol abuse have become a problem. American teens, unlike their European peers, don't learn how to drink gradually, safely and in moderation." As Whelan points out, "though the per-capita consumption of alcohol in France, Spain, and

Portugal is higher than in the United States, the rate of alcoholism and alcohol abuse is lower. A glass of wine at dinner is normal practice. Kids learn to regard moderate drinking as an enjoyable family activity rather than as something they have to sneak away to do. Banning drinking by young people makes it a badge of adulthood—a tantalizing forbidden fruit."[13]

"Binge drinking" has become more popular than ever on college campuses, those havens of desiccated sobriety, if one believes the twenty-one-year-old-drinking-age propaganda. Even at the high-school level, a survey of 15,000 seniors by the University of Michigan found that 30 percent of seniors binge (defined as consuming five or more drinks at a single sitting). The drunkenness that soaks the post-twenty-one-year-old-drinking-age college campus has led University of Colorado Chancellor Roderic B. Park to label it an "epidemic" and propose a "learner's permit"[14] for drinking—a nice try, and a bow to the political realities of the day, for no one wants to provoke the MADD hornets, but the demand of those who want a sane alcohol policy must be no less than the repeal of Liddy Dole's decree.

The phrase "forbidden fruit" comes up time and again, but it is not hackneyed: it is the simple truth. Teen alcohol abuse has not declined as a result of the drinking-age boost. The only difference is that eighteen-year olds who, in the dark and unenlightened age that preceded Secretary Dole's revelation, drank in bars or college rathskellers, now drain their six-packs while cruising the highways and byways. Safety first, as nanny might say.

The law also harmed the small businesses that politicians are always mouthing platitudes about: "it will mean a tremendous loss to our industry"[15] foresaw Scott Wexel, legislative director of New York's United Restaurant, Hotel, and Tavern Association—and hundreds of New York's taverns have closed shop since 1984. But then peddlers of liquor have been cast in the devil's role since the first wave of prohibitionists rolled over our land.

As always, the nannies clutched a sheaf of bogus statistics in their hands. The insurance industry, one of the weightiest lobbyists for Big Brother controls, produced a study claiming that states that had raised their drinking ages to twenty-one over the previous decade had experienced an average 13 percent decrease in fatal nighttime accidents among those drivers whose right to drink had been taken away. Note the crucial word: nighttime, when decreased visibility is a significant factor in automobile accidents.

The studies adduced by the prohibitionists to grease the legislative skids for the drinking-age bill were riddled with holes. Grand claims were made: the chairman of the National Transportation Safety Board predicted that 1,250 young lives would be saved each year by the twenty-one bill. The Presidential Commission on Drunk Driving solemnly assured the President that there existed "evidence of a direct correlation between the minimum drinking age and alcohol-related crashes among the age groups affected."[16]

Not so fast. The "evidence" on which this massive coercion was constructed typically counted all highway crashes, not simply those resulting in deaths; this hopelessly skews the numbers, for it has been well established that many accidents are never reported. The Presidential Commission relied heavily on a "time of day" study which simply noted that "alcohol…is particularly likely to be involved in nighttime fatal crashes."[17] How likely is "particularly likely"? It doesn't say. Nor does it bother to determine the percentage of these fatal nighttime crashes that involve teenage drivers. Moreover, as two respected academics argued at the time to no avail the papers marshalled by the prohibitionists "simply ignore general declines in traffic fatalities, which might be occurring for a variety of reasons other than the imposition of a higher drinking age."[18]

These two debunkers, Jack P. DeSario and Frederic N. Bolotin, political science professors at Case Western Reserve University, conducted their own far more reliable and thorough study of the effects of an increased drinking age. Writing in 1985, Professors DeSario and Bolotin examined alcohol-related traffic fatalities in the fifteen states that had raised their drinking ages between 1979 and 1983. The measurement they used—"the percentage of all traffic fatalities that were classified as alcohol-related for at least two years before and two years after a state raised its drinking age"[19]—avoided the disabling flaws of previous studies. The statistics were calculated for the age group affected by the change in state law, for those under eighteen, those aged twenty-one to twenty-five, and those over twenty-five.

DeSario and Bolotin found "no significant change" in the percentage of alcohol-related fatalities among the affected age groups in thirteen of the fifteen states. Typical was Michigan:

> We found…that the number of alcohol-related deaths among eighteen to twenty-year olds in Michigan declined steadily from 227 two years before to 190 two years after the drinking age was raised from eighteen to twenty-one. However, the *percentage* of fatalities that were alcohol related during that period increased

steadily from 43 percent to 51 percent. This indicates that the decline in the number of alcohol-related deaths simply was part of a general decrease in traffic fatalities. There is no evidence from this that the decline was the result of the increase in the drinking age.[20]

In fact, DeSario and Bolotin found that "the percentage of traffic fatalities that were alcohol-related was consistently highest among the twenty-one-to-twenty-five-year-old group."[21] But MADD has yet to demand a Washington-imposed twenty-five-year-old drinking age.

MADD is busy fighting on other fronts, ostensibly against drunk driving but really, actually, at the core, fighting traditional American liberties. It may not call itself tyrannical, but even its friends see quite clearly what it's up to. The United Nations' World Health Organization has hailed resurgent temperance movements in the United States and elsewhere as marking "a swing...away from complete liberalization and towards a reasonable degree of alcohol control."[22]

What the UN regards as "complete liberty" is unlikely to have impressed Jefferson; when free men and women of his day heard the phrase "reasonable degree of control," they reached for their flintlocks.

Unhappy Hours

Just how reasonable are the new controls? Some are almost self-parodic. H.L. Mencken once defined puritanism as the "haunting fear that someone, somewhere, may be happy." How fitting, then, that the neo-puritans have targeted for elimination those pleasurable occasions known as "happy hours."

The happy hour is a period, usually during late afternoon on a weekday, when a bar serves drinks at reduced prices or offers free hors d'oeuvres. This is a perfectly understandable effort to lure customers in during off-peak hours; yet, to such advocates as Maureen H. Dugan of the New York State Council on Alcoholism, its promotion of "easier access to alcohol" carries with it "costs to society."[23] Dugan's (government-funded) organization was a prime supporter of an unsuccessful attempt to ban happy hours in New York in the 1980s; the bill failed, in part due to the determined opposition of the New York State Restaurant Association.

But those who enjoy a beer and a few handfuls of Chex party mix on the way home from work in other states were not always so lucky. In Kansas, home of Carry Nation, legislators sought to abolish the happy hour in 1985 by mandating that drink prices must remain the same all day long. No problem, said enterprising bar owners: "We didn't get rid of the specials. We just extended happy hours into 'happy days,'" as Ken Wallace, owner of Lawrence's Jay Hawk Cafe, told the *Wall Street Journal*.[24]

The Kansas bluenoses also enjoined "all you can drink" specials: bar owners fought back by charging a penny a drink for those who paid a cover charge. Even ladies' nights, that venerable institution in which women may drink to their hearts' content, free of charge, was on the legislators' hit list. But old-fashioned Middle American ingenuity foiled the best-laid plans of meddling men again. Bars such as the Light House Grog & Galley in Overland Park took to giving each woman who entered a gift of several dollars, to be spent, it was hoped, on libations therein.

The attacks that unhappy persons launch on happy hours reached their *reductio ad absurdum* in Michigan some years back, when lawmakers banned free pretzels from bars. Not to be outdone, prudish bureaucrats in Colorado banned the serving of wine at public art galleries. Just when you think it can't get any worse....

"Open-container" laws are another item on MADD's wish list. In about half the states, drinking while one is driving is permitted, as long as the driver is not intoxicated or driving dangerously. And there is no evidence that a ban on such behavior makes any difference at all, as Clay Hall of the National Highway Traffic Safety Administration admitted. Nevertheless, prohibiting such action by what are known as open-container laws is necessary because "there's nothing worse than driving down the road and seeing someone swigging a can of beer,"[25] said Ann Seymour of MADD. So, naturally, Ms. Seymour's aesthetic preferences must be legislated, even though a ban on listening to loud music while driving would probably do more to promote safety.

Busybodies in Texas have tried to enact open-container laws for years, without much success. The campaign often takes on a class edge: yuppies trying to punish working-class and rural men. Texas State Representative Gary Thompson, a leading nanny in the state legislature in the 1980s, explained his frustration: "It is sacrosanct in Texas because of the frontier mentality that is so much a part of the state. I think it derives from sportsmen who like tooling around in their pickups, or Joe Six-Pack drinking a beer on the way home from work. Those who are against the law will just ask why you are punishing Joe Six-Pack when he's not doing anybody any harm by having a beer on the way home."[26]

Why, indeed, Rep. Thompson? Why prohibit activities that, according to available evidence, are harmless? Like Ann Seymour, Thompson doesn't like seeing working men enjoying themselves in a manner that offends his delicate sensibilities. So the law must be changed.

The toll that drunk driving exacts on the families of victims is incalculable: the loss of a loved one to a reckless drunk is too horrible a possibility for most of us to imagine. Driving while intoxicated is, quite properly, treated as a serious crime in every state of the union. We do not quarrel with the severity of DUI (driving under the influence) or DWI (driving while intoxicated) laws. But MADD and its fraternal neo-prohibitionists want to so expand the definition of driving while under the influence as to render it meaningless; in a MADD MADD world, a diner would not dare to have a beer with his clams, or two glasses of wine with her pasta, for this negligible imbibing would put the not-quite-teetotaller at risk of a drunk-driving arrest and the chain of punishments that follow: loss of drivers' license, hefty fines and lawyer's fees, public disgrace, and possibly imprisonment. So all but the fearless and foolhardy would abstain from spirits except when in the home and even there, in the privacy of one's castle, the Carry Nations would eventually come a-hatcheting…"for the sake of the children."

Creeping Prohibition

Now that twenty-year olds have to sneak bottles of beer like rowdy thirteen-year olds lighting cigarettes in the garage, the next big push of the neo-prohibitionists will be to lower the blood alcohol content or concentration (BAC) definition of drunkenness.

The campaign of Candy Lightner, founder of MADD, led to all fifty states reducing their BAC level, which in most cases had been .15, to .10. Now we are in the process of further reducing it to .08, or almost half its traditional limit. Of course, when the BAC is .08 accidents will still happen; morons will still get drunk and drive cars and kill people. There is simply no way to eliminate drunk driving, though some remedies—particularly license revocation—are more effective than others. Not even Prohibition will do, though if MADD gets its way we will discover this anew.

At this writing, thirty-five states set the BAC level for driving while intoxicated at .10, thirteen have set it at .08, and two states do not define drunkenness in terms of a blood alcohol content. This kind of diversity, this modest variety of standards, is unacceptable to those who know the one true best way to do things. So MADD, naturally, wants Congress to override this traditional state responsibility and mandate a national BAC standard of .08. For starters. Those states that do not buckle under would lose federal highway monies—the same carrot-and-stick routine Washington pulled on the national drinking age.

Several studies have demonstrated that "the relation between risk and BAC is essentially flat until the .08 or .09 level for BAC."[27] Thus reasonable people can argue over whether the BAC cutoff level for driving under the influence should be .08 or .10 but this is *not* MADD's ultimate goal. They will go far beyond sensible reform, into the realm of petty tyranny. Eventually, should the rest of us take leave of our senses and votes, expect a BAC of .02 putting us in a land in which the one-beer lunch, never mind the one-martini lunch, is a musty relic of the carefree past.

Washington has dictated that the states adopt a maximum BAC level of .04 for truckers and drivers of commercial vehicles. There is no doubt that once MADD has persuaded all fifty states to reduce their BAC levels to .08, the next step will be .04. After all, we can hear prohibitionists already: if a .05 BAC level makes the driver of a truck a menace on the road, mustn't that also be true of the driver of an automobile? Cars kill almost as readily as trucks do; do we value our children's lives so little that we permit men who would be arrested as legally drunk if they were behind the wheel of a truck to weave their cars unsteadily through traffic?

Think this is alarmism? Think again. At this writing, thirty-seven states have enacted zero-tolerance laws, under which drivers under the age of twenty-one lose their licenses if they register a BAC level of .02—the equivalent of one beer or glass of wine. (Deliciously, New York's zero-tolerance law was coauthored by Assemblywoman Susan John, a leading prohibitionist and chairwoman of the Assembly's Alcohol and Drug Abuse Committee. Alas, Assemblywoman John was later pulled over in a suburb of Albany, when police observed her car moving erratically, and she was arrested with a BAC that made her legally drunk. True to the finest traditions of hypocrisy, she remains an ardent, if somewhat lower-profile, neo-prohibitionist. RID, among others, has demanded her resignation, but few pols give up power voluntarily.)

It is only a matter of time before zero-tolerance is advanced as an appropriate measure for battling drunk drivers of all ages. The Office for Substance Abuse Prevention has publicly recommended that the legal definition of drunkenness be reduced to a BAC level of .04, which means that if a 140-pound woman drinks two beers and gets behind the wheel, they'll haul her off to jail. In 1993, MADD president Milo Kirk praised Sweden's draconian .02 BAC level. Kirk gazed wistfully at the Scandanavian nanny state: how cursedly unfortunate we are to live in a nation that still has a vestigial respect for individual liberties and the right of a man to act as he pleases, as long as he harms no one. Why can't we be like the Swedes? (Who have one of the highest suicide rates in the world, but we shan't go into that.)

Even MADD's Candy Lightner concedes that a majority of drunken drivers who cause deaths have a BAC of .17 or higher which means that they are blindingly drunk, so far beyond the gray area of .08–.10 as to render the debate almost frivolous. Sociologist H. Laurence Ross points out that there is little difference in the driving performance of those with .08 BAC levels as opposed to .10; neither group is the problem, and lowering the definition of drunken driving "would brand as criminal much behavior that is customary, pleasurable and much less risky to society."[28]

Moreover, lowering the BAC is perhaps the *least* effective way to reduce drunk driving. Powerful evidence comes from the first nationwide survey of driver drinking driver attitudes toward DWI laws.

The survey was conducted in 1992 by Dr. David W. Moore and R. Kelly Myers of the University of New Hampshire Survey Center. Moore and Myers sampled 702 drivers who had, within the past year, operated a motor vehicle within two hours of consuming alcohol. Thus they cut to the pith of matter: they asked drinkers themselves "how likely they are to be deterred from driving under the influence of alcohol by their state anti-drunk driving laws."[29]

The scholars considered five strategies for combating DWI:

- A mandatory jail sentence of at least one week for those convicted of driving under the influence;
- Lowering the blood alcohol content from .10 to .08;
- Automatically revoking the driver's license for one year of anyone convicted of driving under the influence;
- A mandatory fine of $500 for those convicted of driving under the influence; and
- Increasing the price of alcoholic beverages by 10 percent via a tax.

Drivers were asked which of these measures would cause them to drink "much less" when at a tavern. (The pollsters concede that it is far easier to *say* you will cut back on drinking than actually to do it, so the figures testifying to these measures' effectiveness are no doubt inflated.)

According to drinkers themselves, the automatic revocation of a drunk driver's license is by far the most effective measure that a state could take to combat DWI. Fully 40 percent of imbibers said that they would "drink less"[30] were such a law on the books. The other strategies, in declining order of effectiveness, were a mandatory jail sentence, an automatic fine, and, trailing way behind, lowering the blood alcohol content, and increasing the cost of alcohol.

The pollsters next measured the combined deterrent effect of these laws, that is, how much additional deterrence each proposal would provide were the others also in effect. Again, by far the weakest deterrents were dropping the BAC and boosting the price of booze. Adopting the former would deter a bare 2.3 percent of drinkers; the latter would deter an additional 1.0 percent from drinking while driving.

When the sample is narrowed to only those drivers who admitted having driven while drunk over the past year, the results are similar. In combination with the other strategies, lowering the BAC to .08 deters only an additional 1.6 percent of drunk drivers, while levying a 10 percent tax on alcohol deters an additional 3.9 percent. Again, by far the most effective strategy is automatic license revocation.

The authors conjecture that one reason fiddling with the BAC level has so little impact on drunk driving is that drivers, drunk or sober, haven't the foggiest idea what a BAC is or how it is measured. Just 5 percent of the sample accurately guessed the number of drinks consumed that would place one within a BAC range of .08–.12.

This pathbreaking study made absolutely no impression on the neo-prohibitionists, who are usually so fond of flinging statistics about like so much hash. "Raising excise taxes is probably the most effective way to reduce drinking-and-driving fatalities," said Pat Taylor of CSPI shortly before the study appeared, and she has not recanted. "The way we're pricing alcohol now is not good for public health."[31]

The mandatory imprisonment of those convicted of drunk driving, while hailed by some neo-prohibitionists as the best thing since non-alcoholic beer, creates its own problems. The deterrent effects of rigorous DWI enforcement "appear to diminish over time,"[32] as researchers from the National Institute of Justice found. Though these researchers were obviously friendly to stepped-up enforcement, they conceded a host of related complications.

For one thing, costs skyrocket. Court workloads increase; cases are backlogged; and prisons become overcrowded as otherwise nonviolent DWI offenders are thrown in with rapists and thieves and murderers. Defendants contest their cases far more frequently, for who wants to suffer the inhuman treatment of many jails? Probation caseloads explode. The cure: money, money, and more money. More cops, more judges, more prisons, and taxes through the roof. Though we are told that the annual economic loss due to drunk driving accidents ranges from "$21 to $24 billion for property damage alone,"[33] no price tag is slapped on mandatory imprisonment. What is more, the researchers admit that there's no strong evidence that the policy even works! Yes, traffic fatalities have declined in mandatory-incarceration states, but "traffic fatalities began a general decline in 1981, both nationally and in the case-study jurisdictions."[34]

The lack of a demonstrated causal connection between neo-prohibitionism and the long-term downward trend of alcohol-related fatalities is what drives numbers-literate people crazy. The iconoclastic author Nicholas von Hoffman writes, "The rate of death by motor vehicles for young people is lower than it was twenty-five years ago, and yet all we get on television is Mothers Against Drunk Drivers [sic], a worthy cause doubtless, but scarcely an overwhelming one on the basis of these figures. And how do we defend forcing states to change their legal drinking age, bearing in mind that this legislation comes after, not before, the drop in the mortality rates?"[35]

We can't defend it, but that doesn't mean the nannies won't. New Jersey's Senator Frank Lautenberg, who authored the national twenty-one-year-old drinking age, boasts that he "is saving almost 1,100 young lives each and every year,"[36] a hubristic and statistically ignorant claim.

We have to be careful with DWI statistics, and a quick glance at some statistics will show us why. In 1993, of the 40,115 traffic fatalities in the United States, 13,984 involved an intoxicated driver or intoxicated nonoccupant. (This latter category includes, for the most part, drunks who walk into the road and inebriated motorcyclists.) These 13,984 fatalities break down like this:[37]

	Number	Percent
Intoxicated Drivers	7,578	54
Nonintoxicated Drivers	938	7
Passengers	2,917	21
Intoxicated Nonoccupants	1,936	14
Nonintoxicated Nonoccupants	615	4

So in almost two-thirds of cases, drunks may be killing themselves. Which should not surprise us, given that most automobile accidents by

DWI drivers are single-car crashes. We are, in this country, increasingly reluctant to assign fault; to "blame the victim." But let us remember that a majority of the deaths attributable to drunk driving are of the drunks themselves.

The neo-prohibitionist group with the biggest bankroll is the nation's insurers, who would prefer every American to stay in his or her house all day, never use an appliance, and still shell out hefty sums for premiums. If the word "liberty" has ever appeared in an insurance industry publication, rest assured that it was by accident (Liberty Mutual excepted). Typically, a pamphlet of the Insurance Information Institute recommends sobriety checkpoints and greatly increased use of breath analysis machines.[38] Roadblocks—the stopping of *all* drivers on a particular stretch of road on the suspicion that a few may have been drinking are a favorite cause of both MADD and the insurance industry.

Every bit as intolerable to those who love liberty and believe in the fast-fading notion of personal responsibility are those laws that make the drink server liable for any damage that a drunk might do. The court cases issuing from this perversion of personal responsibility are famous for their absurdity. There was the Texas woman whose daughter died after drinking more than twenty shots of tequila. Mom sued the distiller: why was there no warning label on the bottle? How was the poor girl to know that downing twenty-plus shots of tequila might not be a swell idea? (A jury awarded the grieving mother more than one million dollars, though the judgement was overturned by an appeals court.[39]) Then there was the man who sued Anheuser-Busch for $10,000 for false advertising. His claim, paraphrased by David Shaw, was that "television commercials fraudulently led him to believe that if he drank Bud Light, he could enjoy the same kind of fantasy life that was depicted in the commercials featuring 'tropical settings and beautiful women and men engaged in unrestricted merriment.'"[40] The courts did not buy it, though they have bought slightly less frivolous claims. Bartenders serving one drink too many to a man who then goes out and runs over some innocent have been deemed liable as though the drunk is not responsible for his own criminal conduct. Flip Wilson used to say that the devil made him do it; feckless drunks can now say, with mounting legal backing, that the barkeep made them do it.

If a bottle of beer cost $75, there would be no barkeeps, and no drunks, and no accidents, and no death, and we'd all live happily and soberly in the Brave New World. At least that is the way the nannies see it. Witness their persistent lobbying for excise taxes, on the apparent grounds that if it is potable, tax it.

Even in the wake of independence, when our land was flush with freedom, when American liberty was at its high-water mark, the controllers lurked in the wings. In 1791, the College of Physicians of New York recommended to the U.S. Senate that it place high duties on imported alcohol to discourage consumption. Two-hundred-plus years later, the same refrain is sung by Those Who Know Best. Excise taxes—internal taxes levied on commodities, in this case beer, wine, and spirituous liquors are their favorite song.

The inevitable Michael Jacobson grabs a megaphone every year at budget time to proclaim inanely, "Take your pick. Either demolish programs like the Small Business Administration, Medicare or school lunches for children or raise excise taxes on alcoholic beverages."[41]

Indeed, "higher taxes on alcoholic beverages" can "help greatly in reducing the deficit."[42] (Not exactly: all alcohol excise taxes combined account for less than 1 percent of federal revenue. And in other publications, CSPI recommends that the monies raised by "substantial" tax hikes be applied not to budget-deficit reduction but to "fund prevention, treatment, and research programs"[43] in what promises to be an ever-bulging circle of tax boosts to fund the therapeutic state. And though CSPI worships Washington with a fervor that Christians would call idolatrous, the fifty states are encouraged to get in on the action, too. "Ignoring low alcohol tax rates serves only to…deny state governments a valuable source of additional revenue."[44])

It's all very well for Mr. Jacobson to be so concerned about the continued health of the welfare state, but he's got cards he ain't showing, as the old song goes. For what he and the neo-prohibitionists really want are prohibitively high levies on demon rum and succubus beer.

Fortunately for the beer drinkers of America, those politicians who still have a residual loyalty to the working class are reluctant to vote for a beer tax, seeing it, properly, as a regressive tax that hits working people the hardest. A Congressional Budget Office study of the mid-1980s found that a beer tax hike hit families with incomes of $10–$20,000 three times as hard as it hit families with incomes exceeding $50,000. Additional taxes of up to one dollar per six-pack are blithely bandied about in nanny-land—the higher the better.

Not that this regressivity bothers our betters. "It's true that these taxes are somewhat regressive," sniffs Joseph A. Pechman of the Brookings Institution, "but I think poor people should be discouraged from smoking and drinking."[45] Mr. Pechman does not say whether his habits or vices (no doubt they are much more ennobling than those of blue-collar folks) should likewise be "discouraged" by Washington. Well, you know what sort of people go to tractor pulls.

Moreover, the beer tax particularly wallops smaller breweries and those that compete by underpricing the big boys. George Thompson, an analyst at Prudential-Bache Securities, says of a beer tax, "The ones that will get impacted most significantly are the weaker links. If you put it on those brands that sell purely on price, the tax is a big negative."[46]

It's easy for the well-paid Manhattan twits who write editorials for the *New York Times* to editorialize, as they have, in favor of adding an additional $1.50 to the price of a six-pack of beer. They don't drink the stuff. It shan't beggar them. The Beer Institute claims that almost half—43 percent—of the cost of a bottle of beer is the result of federal and state taxes. Thus, those who wish to lighten the tax burden on American workers ought to clamor not for higher excise taxes but for their repeal. (Fat chance: MADD would hit you harder than a double kamikaze.)

It is accepted as a truism by editorial writers that excise taxes discourage consumption and, in so doing, contribute to the collective health of the citizenry. If those beer-bellied proles can't take care of themselves, well, by golly, we'll take care of them. But neither of these assumptions is necessarily true.

Of course, the folks who actually sell alcohol to a willing audience know that taxes, unless exorbitant, will deter few drinkers. "Prohibition didn't stop them from drinking," Michael Meeks, assistant manager of the Chalet on Chicago's North Side told the *New York Times*. "I don't think taxes are going to stop them, either."[47]

Chimed in Bob Back, manager of a Bell Liquors in Chicago, "I don't think the price increase will make people drink less. It just might change what they drink."[48]

But even if we concede that taxes do discourage consumption, we are left with what University of California-Davis economist Dale M. Heien calls "the paradox of alcohol taxation": "Although it is well known that excessive drinkers often have major health problems, it is less well known that moderate drinkers have above-average health, above the average of both abusers and abstainers alike."[49] (There is, of course, no way to determine at the point of sale when the tax is collected whether the purchaser is a liver-destroying alkie or a health-enhancing moderate drinker.)

We might also consider what Jefferson said: "I think it is a great error to consider a heavy tax on wines as a tax on luxury. On the contrary, it is a tax on the health of our citizens."

For folks who seemingly reduce everything to a cost-benefit ratio (the benefits of state regulation always outweighing the costs of freedom lost), the prohibitionists tiptoe around unwelcome numbers. For instance, researchers using the 1988 Health Interview Survey "estimated the per capita medical care costs for all drinkers to be $3,295 versus $4,430 for nondrinkers."[50] Have a glass of wine and save the taxpayers a few bucks? (For that matter, few policies drained the U.S. Treasury quite as much as Prohibition, which eliminated "a significant source of tax revenue and greatly increased government spending."[51])

The Health Benefits of Booze

The link between good health and the moderate consumption of alcohol, particularly wine, is well-established, though as we will see in Chapter Five, some truths are unsayable in the land of the free.

Every day brings more evidence that a glass (even a tankard) a day keeps the doctor away. Circulatory problems, heart disease, cholesterol, arterial disease: moderate intake of alcohol is no panacea, but it sure helps. Yet temperance attitudes die hard. When in 1997 researchers from Brigham and Women's Hospital and Harvard, writing in *Circulation*, a journal of the American Heart Association, announced their finding that men who had one or two drinks a day had a 32 percent lower risk of hardening of the arteries in the legs, the story was typically framed by patronizing quotes from medical nannies telling us not to "take up drinking" just because...well, just because it's been found to be good for you. "Nondrinkers shouldn't take up drinking," cautioned one of the authors of the study, Dr. Charles H. Hennekens of Harvard Medical School.[52]

But why not? If those at risk of colon disease are advised to adopt a high-fiber diet, why shouldn't those at risk of arterial disease start quaffing a glass of wine at dinnertime? Why is alcohol accorded a moral station somewhere between child pornography and tossing empty beer cans out the car window?

The grape has even been linked to reduced incidence of cancer. Writing in *Science* in 1997, a research team led by John Pezzuto of the University of Illinois at Chicago found that a substance in grapes called resveratrol prevents cells from turning cancerous and also discourages the spread of malignancies. "Of all the plants we've tested for cancer chemopreventive activity and all the compounds we've seen, this one has the greatest promise,"[53] Pezzuto said.

In an earlier study at Oxford University, researchers tracked 19,000 men over thirteen years. Their finding: moderate drinkers had lower death rates than abstainers for *all* diseases, including cancer.

Scaling the heights of political incorrectness, in 1995 researchers concluded a twelve-year study of 13,285 Danish men and women with the finding that "the greatest benefit in terms of longevity came from drinking three to five glasses of wine a day."[54] The stateside implication should be clear: we Americans drink far too little. Per capita wine consumption in these United States is just 1.9 gallons a year; in France, Italy, and Portugal, per-capita ingestion exceeds 15 gallons a year. Americans: *start drinking!*

This is unsayable, except by a few courageous researchers and who-gives-a-damn iconoclasts. Cornell University's Leroy Creasy recommends "drinking red wines [with] every dinner for the rest of your life."[55] Don't expect the Office for Substance Abuse Prevention to highlight that quote in its next propaganda package. Nor will it advertise the study of almost 4,000 elderly people in southwest France which found that the grape thwarted Alzheimer's disease. And we're not talking about a sip now and then, or the "one glass, maximum," that ultracautious doctors may recommend. No, these researchers found that among those who imbibed two to four glasses of wine a day, "dementia was slowed by 80 percent and Alzheimer's was slowed by 75 percent in those showing symptoms." Of course the stateside news item reporting this remarkable finding lectured, "the researchers aren't advising elderly people to start [drinking]."[56] Well, *why not?*

The drinking age, bartender-liability laws, open-container proscriptions, altering BAC levels, the abolition of happy hour: many Americans see these as piecemeal violations of liberty, they concede, but nothing to get alarmed about. After all, the sale and manufacture of alcohol is still legal, and the Twenty-first Amendment settled the larger question for all time.

But after a while, as piece after piece is added to the puzzle, a pattern begins to take shape. A pattern that we have seen before. Leave it to the impolitic purists to admit what we are really seeing. The Prohibition Party's 1996 platform, upon which the non-juggernaut ticket of Dodge and Kelly stood, declared:

We are encouraged by the nationwide legal drinking age of twenty-one, the sharp decline in booze sales, plus a 44 percent abstinence rate in America. Alcohol is still America's number one drug problem, causing death to over 400,000 Americans each year due to accidents, homicides and health problems. It is the chief cause of poverty, broken homes, juvenile and adult crime, political corruption and wasted manpower in the United States.

The liquor industry is linked to and supports a nationwide network of gambling, vice, and crime. It exercises a large measure of control over the two major political parties and much of the governmental life of our nation. Our party alone offers a program of publicity, education, legislation and administration leading to the prohibition of the manufacturing, distribution and sale of all alcoholic beverages. Americans already believe in prohibition (LSD, cocaine, heroin, etc.). We will help Americans to realize that alcohol's harmful effects far outweigh those of all illegal drugs combined.[57]

The programs and plans of the national nannies, whatever their acronyms, and however much they doth protest that the P-word is the farthest thing from their minds, lead to prohibition. This is the road we are on, though only the elderly zealots of a once-significant, now-obscure fringe political party are honest enough to say it.

5

Free Speech: You Gotta Be Kidding!

*Speech is civilization itself. The word, even
the most contradictory word, preserves
contact; it is silence which isolates.*
—Thomas Mann, *The Magic Mountain*

The First Amendment to the Constitution of the United States reads, in full, "Congress shall make no law respecting an establishment of religion, or prohibiting the free exercise thereof; or abridging the freedom of speech, or of the press; or the right of the people peaceably to assemble, and to petition the Government for a redress of grievances."

The language is clear, blessedly free of the beclouding legalisms that obscure many contemporary statutes. So let's say I own a small winery in California's Napa Valley or New York's Finger Lakes region. In designing my labels, do I have the right to include factual and well-documented claims about the healthful qualities of my product? Of course I do if the First Amendment is still in effect, which, last time we checked, it was.

But maybe we should check again. For we do not have that right. Until very recently vintners could not assert any "therapeutic or curative" qualities for their potables. We may be on the cusp of a weakening of this proscription or it may just be a temporary lull before the next prohibitionist storm.

The salubrious effects of moderate drinking are common knowledge in European nations, and while Americans have learned of them through a kind of homegrown samizdat folk wisdom passed on across fences and over water coolers, the nanny state will have none of it. *60 Minutes*, the CBS-television investigative show, has twice asked the question, "Why do the oenophilic French, diets larded with fat, have lower rates of cardiovascular disease than Americans?" And the answer? Dr.

Serge Renaud of Lyons Centre told the unsinkable Morley Safer: "There is no other drug that's been so efficient [in preventing heart disease] as a moderate intake of alcohol."[1] (One *60 Minutes* report inspired a virtual run on red wine: supermarkets reported a 40 percent jump in sales.)

Wine (particularly red wine) can be one of your cardiovascular system's best friends, though you'd never know it if you relied on the health-and-safety mandarins of the U.S. government.

BATF: All Fired up Like at Waco

Ominously, the agency responsible for regulating alcoholic beverage labels is the Bureau of Alcohol, Tobacco and Firearms (BATF), the folks who brought you Waco in all its incinerated glory. Fresh from the massacre of religious dissenters in that Texas field, the BATF trained its guns (this time metaphorical, thank God) on those merchants and wine-sellers so naive as to think they might advertise wine's beneficial effects on their labels.

As Ben Lieberman of the Competitive Enterprise Institute puts it:

> More than 100 studies establishing the connection between moderate alcohol consumption and substantial reductions in cardiovascular risk and overall mortality have appeared in the *New England Journal of Medicine*, the *Journal of the American Medical Association*, the *British Medical Journal*, and others. Among medical researchers, the facts are no longer in doubt. But the ATF bureaucrats who regulate alcoholic beverage labels and advertisements can't handle the truth. They don't want the public to know that there could be anything good about drinking."[2]

Though the Bureau has yet to raid *Falconcrest* or take hostages at family wineries, it has been, as is its wont, insensible of the usual American freedoms. As reported by the *Los Angeles Times*, the BATF once "ordered tiny Leeward Winery of Ventura to recall a newsletter in which its winemaker discussed the [*60 Minutes*] program."[3]

The Competitive Enterprise Institute (CEI) has been a mischievous thorn in the BATF's side. The CEI distributed mock wine labels for "Vino Veritas Freedom of Speech Wine." (How refreshing to see a civil-liberties group with a CSPI-like knack for goofy publicity stunts!) Few phrases so irritate the nanny state as much as "freedom of speech," which remains a hoary ideal to which even the most dedicated censor must pay homage. So while CEI has yet to earn a visit from BATF's finest, vino has yet to win the right to speak veritas. The Institute has also created labels for "Stout Heart," the "Freedom of Speech Beer." Both beer and wine labels state, "There is significant evidence that moderate consumption of alcoholic beverages may reduce the risk of heart disease," an incontrovertible statement that BATF controverts. Or not so much controverts as simply censors. CEI, along with Consumer Alert, is suing the BATF to force it to require that wine labels list *both the risks and the benefits* of wine consumption.

There have been small but not insignificant advances: the first occurred in 1992, when the Bureau approved a Beringer Vineyards wine bottle "neckhanger" which included six paragraphs from the notorious *60 Minutes* broadcast. Others followed, but this was hardly an unalloyed victory, for as BATF spokesman Tom Hill noted, such labels must also state that "drinking may be harmful."[4] Health statements are automatically rejected by the BATF "unless they are properly qualified, present all sides of the issue, and outline the categories of individuals for whom any positive effects would be outweighed by numerous negative health effects."[5] The BATF concedes that it is "extremely unlikely that such a balanced claim would fit on a normal alcoholic beverage label,"[6] so what at first glance seemed to be an unwonted act of leniency by BATF is no more than a bureaucratic shell game. Lawsuits are pending and perhaps the Supreme Court will someday strike down this patently unconstitutional form of speech control, but how many of us will succumb to heart disease in the meantime—heart disease which can be ameliorated by a glass or two of wine a day?

The Competitive Enterprise Institute commissioned a poll in 1995 which asked, "Do you believe that scientific evidence exists showing that moderate consumption of alcohol, approximately one or two drinks per day, may reduce the risk of heart disease for many people?"[7] A bare plurality—41.7 to 38.1 percent—answered yes as opposed to no, and fully 20.2 percent did not know. Only 9.7 percent knew that all alcohol not merely, say, red wine can be beneficial.

Thus, fewer than one in ten Americans knows the truth about moderate alcohol consumption and health—a lack of awareness that is truly startling, and would not be tolerated by the nanny state for one second were the subject tobacco. CEI General Counsel Sam Kazman charged, "BATF is directly responsible for fostering this state of ignorance with a policy that flatly violates the First Amendment." Kazman adds, "BATF is preventing consumers from receiving truthful, useful information. This policy is illogical from the standpoint of public health, and illegal from the standpoint of the First Amendment. It's one thing to be barred from falsely shouting 'fire' in a crowded theater. It's quite another story when you can't say 'L'Chaim!' (To Life!) in a liquor store."[8]

The manifold benefits of fiber were largely unknown to the public until labels got the word out: the healthy effects of wine and other alcohol have yet to really penetrate the public consciousness, in large part because the BATF regards Americans as dolts unable to process information unless it has been fed into a bureaucratic blender and reduced to pablum. In response to a letter from Consumer Alert, BATF functionary James Crandall claims that permitting alcoholic beverage labels to inform consumers of their contents' salubrious qualities would "mislead" the American Republic. "Even if backed up by medical evidence," writes Crandall, such a statement misleads if it "is not properly qualified, does not give all sides of the issue, and does not outline the categories of individuals for whom any such positive effect would be outweighed by numerous negative health effects."[9] Crandall and the BATF don't want a label, they want a book. (And speaking of "all sides of the issue," where are the statements on cigarette labels testifying to the pleasurable qualities that so many find in the satanic stick?)

Even the Department of Health and Human Services and the U.S. Department of Agriculture, in their *Dietary Guidelines for Americans*, have acknowledged that "current evidence suggests that moderate drinking is associated with a lower risk for coronary heart disease in some individuals." The BATF itself, in an industry circular of 8 August 1993, admitted that "there is a growing body of evidence that lower levels of drinking decrease the risk of death from coronary artery disease."[10] But the bureau is dragging its feet on the matter, and the old reliables are keeping up the caterwaul.

"It would be foolhardy to offer a prescription for increased alcohol consumption as official government policy,"[11] declaimed George Hacker, director of alcohol policies (e.g., prohibition in all but name) at CSPI. C. Everett Koop has chimed in, per usual, in his role as admiral of abstemiousness.

The K Street paternalists are no less tenacious in defense of the warning labels that federal law (another Reagan-era innovation) requires on bottles of hootch. The first half of this admonition states, "According to the Surgeon General, women should not drink alcoholic beverages during pregnancy because of the risk of birth defects." This flat, unequivocal, unqualified statement is in fact a contentious issue in the medical community; in *Alcohol and the Fetus*, Dr. Henry Rosett and Lyn Weiner of Boston University write that "the recommendation that all women should abstain from drinking during pregnancy is not based on scientific evidence, since no risks have been observed from small quantities."[12] In *Reason*, Jacob Sullum quotes Harvard University's Dr. Jack Mendelson that "it is possible that some doses of alcohol, low or moderate, may improve the probability for health pregnancies and healthy offspring."[13]

"Both sides of the issue," anyone?

Viewers of television don't even get one side of the issue when it comes to liquor, which, due to the industry's Code of Good Practice, had never been advertised on television until Seagram broke the forty-eight-year silence in June 1996.

Seagram and other members of the Distilled Spirits Council of the United States (DISCUS) had, since 1936, agreed not to advertise on radio; in 1948, this self-silencing practice was extended to the infant medium of television.

Members of DISCUS have long chafed under this restraint, and understandably so: beer-makers and vintners fill the airwaves with their commercials, and just why malt liquor should fall in fair grounds while distilled liquor is out of bounds gave cause for ferment. So in March 1996, Seagram aired an ad for Crown Royal blended scotch whiskey on the Prime Sports cable network, and the sky did not fall. By June of that year it was airing commercials in Corpus Christi, Texas. That fall it expanded to such markets as Boston, Houston, and San Francisco. Chivas Regal scotch and Lime Twisted gin were also hawked. No increase in DWI fatalities or epidemics of looting and pillaging by men, intoxicated senseless by Crown Royal, were reported in any of the affected cities, but the very thought that demon whiskey was appearing on the pure-as-driven-snow television screens of America made the nannies apoplectic.

Congressman Joseph P. Kennedy II (D-Mass.), namesake of his bootlegging grandpa, introduced legislation to ban liquor ads. "Do the right thing," the ever-sober, saintly, and jesuitical President Clinton urged the distillers in his weekly national radio address, "... get back to the ban, and pull those ads."[14] The usual full-page ad coordinated by CSPI appeared in the *New York Times* (this one had the obligatory rainbow coalition of children half-submerged in a liquor bottle).

The Seagram ads constituted a "powerful inducement to drink,"[15] declared CSPI front group, the Coalition for the Prevention of Alcohol Problems (CPAP) by banning alcohol, honesty ought to compel it to add. (One member of the Coalition, by the way, is the National Women's Christian Temperance Union.) Yet this statement by CPAP is manifestly and empirically untrue.

"Nobody has been able to demonstrate that advertising does anything more than shift brand preferences. It surely doesn't increase consumption,"[16] Washington University sociologist David J. Pittman told Jacob Sullum, and indeed this was the conclusion of a 1985 study by the Senate Subcommittee on Alcohol and Drug Abuse. (Meanwhile, CPAP pipes: "There is no proof that there is not a link between alcohol advertising and consumption."[17] Sure, just because 5,001 studies have shown no link doesn't mean that the 5,002nd won't find one....)

CSPI propaganda sheets blanch in horror because beer and wine ads depict "the normalcy of drinking."[18] Precisely. Because moderate drinking *is* "normal" to most Americans. Indeed, children raised in an environment in which moderate drinking is accepted are less likely to fall prey to the "forbidden fruit" syndrome; alcohol is not a temptress, the agency of their downfall, but simply a minor part of everyday life. To CSPI, commercials have so warped young minds that "more than a quarter of high school seniors do not view having one or two drinks nearly every day as entailing great risk of harm."[19] The wonder is that this perceptive quarter discovered the truth, despite the swamp of prohibitionist vapor they encounter in school.

"Just because there's no law against it doesn't make it right,"[20] whines CPAP. The problem, dear Coalition, is that you *demand* that we do make a law against it. This hypocrisy runs through the literature of the nanny groups on the subject of advertising. "Health messages on alcohol ads will not ban advertising for alcoholic beverages," says one Coalition publication. "Health messages in ads will provide much-needed public health information about the use of America's number-one drug. This is consistent with the free speech philosophy of providing more information, rather than censoring speech."[21]

Oh, joy: nanny discovers the First Amendment. But what hogwash! For later in the same lobbying packet, the Coalition urges "restricting or even banning commercial speech."[22] So much for "the free speech philosophy of providing more information, rather than censoring speech."

The goal is obvious: banning all advertisements for anything stronger than fruit punch as the first step toward the re-establishment of American prohibition. Michael Jacobson has spoken casually of "eliminating"[23] alcohol ads. Beware activists who toss around words like "eliminate": as the old Creedence Clearwater Revival song went, "sooner or later they'll point the cannon at you."

No whisper of booze is too slight to escape nanny's attention. The chronic meddlers of CSPI protested the appearance of the Anheuser-

Busch Clydesdales in President Clinton's first inaugural parade. The State of Washington Department of Health was so worried that the moronic "Bud Bowl" commercials broadcast during the Super Bowl were giving kids the wrong message—drink beer and you, too, can be a brown translucent bottle!—that it used taxpayers' money to buy counter-ads. A particularly fanatical teetotaler named Dr. Trisha Roth, known as the Carry Nation of Beverly Hills, squealed to authorities on forty restaurants and other places *including her own synagogue* for failing to post state-mandated anti-alcohol signs.[24] And on it goes.

Indeed, BATF regulators look like bleeding heart civil libertarians when compared to the FDA and those certain congresspeople who are never so busy sucking up to moneybags lobbyists that they can't find time for cheap moralistic C-SPAN grandstanding. Case in point: the strange tale of Crazy Horse Malt Liquor.

Going Crazy over Crazy Horse

Crazy Horse was a heroic warrior of the Oglala Lakota: the Sioux nation. That much we can all agree on. But when a small New York brewery named Hornell produced a Crazy Horse Malt Liquor (companion to Jim Bowie Pilsner and Annie Oakley Lite), the brewers could be forgiven for thinking that they had stumbled into another Wounded Knee.

Paternalistic whites played the role of the U.S. cavalry: the most hilariously cast was Congressman Joseph Kennedy (D-Mass.). As James Bovard noted in the *Wall Street Journal*, the sanctimonious Kennedy's "inherited wealth stemmed largely from his grandfather's bootleg racket."[25] Nevertheless, Kennedy demanded that Crazy Horse be pulled from the market—never mind the many other "alcoholic beverages named after Indians and Indian tribes, such as Thunderbird wine, Black Hawk Stout, and Chief Osh-Kosh Red Lager."[26]

The BATF actually approved the Crazy Horse label. As its squirming factotum William T. Earle told a congressional committee on 19 May 1992, "With regard to 'Crazy Horse' brand malt liquor, the [Federal Alcohol Administration] Act specifically prohibits the use of a brand name that is the name of any living individual of public prominence, if the use of that name is likely to mislead the consumer into believing that the product has been endorsed, made, or used by that individual. However, there is no prohibition on the use of the name of a deceased historical figure, such as Crazy Horse."[27]

Earle did assure the committee that the BATF had "strongly urged the brand owners to take a more responsible approach,"[28] and when the BATF "urges," prudent men gulp and obey. But the owners of Hornell Brewing Company, John Ferolito and Don Vultaggio, were ex-New York beer-truck drivers, a type not noted for cowardly acquiescence. They refused to change the name of their beer.

The congressional hearing featured a parade of white bureaucrats and members of the Sioux nation demanding Hornell's head on a plate. The Native American witnesses made some compelling, or at least arguable, points; the chief white witness, Surgeon General Antonia C. Novello, did not.

Novello never really found her footing as Surgeon General; she lacked the striking mien and cool beard of her predecessor, C. Everett Koop, and it is the rare man or woman indeed who can wear that absurd Surgeon General uniform without looking like Captain Kangaroo. Antonio Novello was not a rare woman.

The Surgeon General, evincing that underestimation of Americans' intelligence for which our bureaucrats are famous, worried that the popularity of the film *Dances with Wolves* would spur impressionable youths to drain the contents of bottles just because an Indian is on the label. She referred euphemistically to "the alcohol-related challenges"[29] faced by Native Americans . This was a laughably p.c. formulation of a very real problem: the high rates of alcoholism (six times that of the general population) found in the Native American population.

Surgeon General Novello is also one of the few people on this planet to regard the BATF as excessively liberal. She complained that it had approved the Crazy Horse label adding, that the Bureau "can only reject a label if it is false, disparaging, deceptive or misleading. I personally feel that this product indeed fits that characterization."[30] And how, we might ask? Well, she didn't have quite enough time in her statement to answer that. The front of the label featured a depiction of a proud Native American and the words "The Original Crazy Horse Malt Liquor" and "Product of America." Hard to spot the lie there. And surely the Surgeon General's objection was not to the back label, which read:

The Black Hills of Dakota, steeped in the history of the American West, home of Proud Indian Nations.

A land where imagination conjures up images of blue clad Pony Soldiers and magnificent Native American Warriors.

A land still rutted with the wagon tracks of intrepid pioneers.

A land where wailful winds whisper of Sitting Bull, Crazy Horse and Custer.

A land of character, of bravery, of tradition.

A land that truly speaks of the spirit that is America.[31]

Where, precisely, is the untruth here?

Of course, there is none. The Surgeon General also scored the president of Hornell for saying that "growth in the industry has been fastest in ethnic markets in major cities, and, we will go where the market is."[32] Obviously. But in the brave new world of the prohibitionists, marketing your product to people who wish to buy it is sinister just as marketing it to people who have never tried it before (as with cigarettes) is also evil. The manufacturer trying to make a living just can't win.

Hornell refused to sell Crazy Horse in fourteen states with high Native American populations, but the publicity given this witch-hunt created a lively black market for the forbidden malt liquor. In South Dakota, smuggled bottles were fetching $14—five times the retail price.

And it was from South Dakota that the only legitimate criticism of Crazy Horse Malt Liquor came. Several members of the Sioux Tribe testified at the House hearing. They pointed out that the original Crazy Horse "was a spiritual leader of the Lakota Nation and was strongly opposed to the use of intoxicating beverages or spirits."[33] Placing his name on a malt liquor dishonored his memory, they argued, and Hornell ought to remove it for that reason. Gregg Bourland, chairman of the Cheyenne River Sioux Tribe, asked members to "imagine the outcry from the black community if a brewer were to market a liquor entitled Martin Luther King Beer. Or from the Christian community for a Jesus Christ White Wine."[34]

Mr. Bourland had a point worthy of discussion. Certainly in a free nation Hornell has the *right* to name its malt liquor Crazy Horse or Jesus Christ, for that matter; but in the interests of taste and decency and respect for others, perhaps it should not. But ethical matters were quite beyond the scope of the House hearing. The question at hand was whether the full power of the federal government should be brought to bear against Hornell, and on that there was little dissent. The answer from the committee was a resounding Yes.

Catholic University Professor of Law Robert A. Destro did offer a word of warning: not only is "regulating speech in order to preserve a specific community's sense of its own culture and religion...fraught with both vagueness and overbreadth concerns," but regulating "the content of otherwise valid commercial speech in order to achieve what are essentially religious or cultural purposes goes to the heart of the First Amendment's Speech, Press and Religion Clause."[35] But this was bad form on Professor Destro's part, bringing up the First Amendment just when all these whiter-than-white lawmakers were congratulating themselves on their sensitivity to Native American concerns, and so Destro, the last person to testify, was duly ignored.

Two weeks later Frank Wolf (R-Va.) offered an amendment to bar brewers from naming alcoholic beverages after dead people. As James Bovard writes, "Mr. Wolf's amendment mortified Boston Beer Co., since it would have outlawed Samuel Adams beer."[36] The House eventually approved a narrower amendment that forbade the issuance of Crazy Horse labels; congressional conferees effectively murdered Crazy Horse. Since 1992, the year of the great Crazy Horse flare-up, alcoholism rates for Native Americans have remained at astronomically high levels. So what did the prohibitionists accomplish? A few headlines, a chance to feel good in the role of the Great White Father/Mother acting solicitously toward the red man, and that's about it.

The Surgeon General may be a nag without a thimbleful of respect for basic American liberties, but at least keeping malt liquor off the market never killed anyone—unlike the FDA, whose cumbrous drug-approval process and heavy-handed regulatory policies have kept potential life-saving drugs off the market for years. The FDA approval process, which is about as comprehensible as a John Cage composition, routinely takes from five to fifteen years and tens of millions, sometimes several hundreds of millions of dollars, before pills—lifesavers, in some cases—are declared vendible.

The FDA's Assault on Free Speech

The Food, Drug and Insecticide Administration was created in 1928; three years later they dropped the bugs, and the FDA was off and running. New drugs could not be sold in interstate commerce without FDA approval; as with most agencies, it added powers by a steady process of accretion, until the FDA's bailiwick came to include "everything in our food supply except meat and poultry, all prescription and nonprescription drugs, cosmetics, breast implants, the nation's blood supply and prescription drugs used to treat animals."[37] The FDA has regulatory power over $1 trillion worth of products; in a not atypical ten-day period in 1995, "the agency approved a new AIDS drug, issued new rules on food safety, approved the first treatment for Lou Gehrig's disease, and banned nighttime laser shows in Las Vegas."[38]

And on the seventh day the FDA rested.

The right to regulate speech is not among the FDA's enumerated powers, but that has not stopped the pill police from doing an Orwellian number on medical dissenters.

Like all government agencies, the FDA views unorthodoxy the way a dentist regards a cavity. When the famed psychoanalyst Dr. Wilhelm Reich marketed his "orgone boxes," and claimed that they could cure everything this side of a runny nose, the FDA struck. Economic journalist Mary Bennett Peterson explains, "The FDA believed the orgone boxes came under the Food, Drug and Cosmetic Act inclusion of medical devices, and therefore moved against Dr. Reich. But the devices were not the only target of the FDA. Dr. Reich's writings were also targets. Interpreting the Act to construe the Reich books as directions and inspirations for the use of the devices, the FDA got a court injunction not only to bar the devices from interstate commerce and prohibit the sale of Reich's works, but to destroy all documents, bulletins, pamphlets, journals, and booklets of Reich's research foundation. In compliance with the injunction, an FDA inspector went to Dr. Reich's office in July 1956 and, in the psychiatrist's presence, burned his books. According to the FDA inspector, Dr. Reich was most pleasant and said that 'his books had been burnt in Germany, and he did not think it would ever happen again, but here they were being burned once again.' Dr. Reich refused to obey the injunction and wound up in a federal penitentiary where he died after seventeen months."[39]

It could have been worse, we suppose: the good doctor might have tried to sell orgone beer, in which case the solicitous boys of the BATF would have paid him a visit, burning not only Reich's writings but Reich himself. (Though "Reich was asking for it," we'd have been assured by the Attorney General after a thorough sifting of the embers.)

The orgone box may be long gone, but the Food and Drug Administration lives on, seemingly eternal, ever vigilant in its crusade to protect the American people against an overdose of information. Heaven forfend that consumers make decisions on their own.

It was not supposed to be this way. At the dawn of the consumer movement, the spread of information and protection against fraud were its laudable purposes. Absolute safety was impossible, and everyone knew it; as Dwight D. Eisenhower once said, "If all Americans want is security, they can go to prison."[40]

Much of what once went by the name of "consumerism" was unobjectionable. Presidents Kennedy and Nixon spelled out the right of consumers in messages of 1962 and 1969, respectively, and it is hard to quarrel with their hackneyed content. It is also hard to detect any similarity between these principles and the demands of CSPI and the rest of our *fin de siècle* nannydom.

President Kennedy asserted that consumers possessed:

- The right to safety. Products should not harm or damage the user and should perform according to manufacturers' claims;
- The right to be informed. Complete and accurate product information should be provided;
- The right to choose. Consumer choice should be preserved, based on the right to choose a diverse number of products; and
- The right to be heard. The consumer viewpoint should be given greater consideration by producers of goods and services.[41]

Nixon's "Buyer's Bill of Rights" was almost identical, perhaps validating those radical critics who in 1960 charged that the presidential election was between handsome Tweedledum and six-o'clock-shadow Tweedledee. President Nixon declared:

- I believe that the buyer in America today has the right to make an intelligent choice among products and services;
- The buyer has the right to accurate information on which to make his free choice;
- The buyer has the right to expect that his health and safety is taken into account by those who seek his patronage; and
- The buyer has the right to register his dissatisfaction, and have his complaint heard and weighed, when his interests are badly served.[42]

Yesterday's "accurate information" became today's "total ban on...." Unelected bureaucrats flexed their new muscle; encountering little resistance, they pushed on, leading to the current situation, in which know-it-alls carry themselves with an in-your-face attitude that could teach NBA power forwards a thing or two.

Even restaurant menus fall within the purview of today's FDA, thanks to a federal district court judge's ruling in the summer of 1996. U.S. District Court Judge Paul L. Friedman ruled that the Nutrition Labeling and Education Act of 1990 covered menus as well as grocery-store foods; as a result, your local greasy spoon or four-star French restaurant cannot use such phrases as "light," "low-fat," or "heart-healthy" without inviting the scrutiny of the no doubt soon-to-be-established Division of Menu Regulation of that federal government that we are being told is shrinking every day.

The Center for Science in the Public Interest was party to the lawsuit—surprise! Its legal director, Bruce Silverglade, asserted, "A restaurant menu should not be a work of fiction."[43] Well, of course it shouldn't; if you order toast and eggs, you should get toast and eggs, not pancakes. If the combo is advertised as "the most delicious toast and eggs you've ever eaten," most Americans over the age of ten realize that a certain charming hyperbole, of justifiable pride, or old-fashioned hucksterism is at work. If in fact the toast is soggy and the eggs leaden, you're not going to sue the diner for fraud, though you may not eat there again. Similarly, a turkey burger advertised as "low fat" almost assuredly is lower in fat than, say, a cheeseburger, but the locution admits of a certain ambiguity. The claim is not false—it does not allege "X grams from fat" when the burger provides Y grams from fat—but it contains the same measure of imprecision as most of our everyday claims. "How do you feel today?" "Oh, pretty good." Should Washington create a Melancholy Measure by which your answer is gauged? Should you be forbidden from saying "pretty good" unless you score above thirty-five on a test devised by the Department of Happiness?

Nonprofit voluntary health agencies, such as the American Heart Association, might be the logical alternative to the FDA as a source of information (the Good Housekeeping Seal of Approval still means more than most "Government Approved" stamps) but the voluntary health agencies (VHAs) have displayed a decided incompetence at coordinating such programs. (See our books *Unhealthy Charities: Hazardous to Your Health and Wealth* and *Cancerscam: Diversion of Federal Cancer Funds to Politics* for critical and detailed investigations into how VHAs, most of which are heavily subsidized by Washington, have sold their souls for money and power.)

When in the late 1980s the American Heart Association announced the HeartGuide seal, under which the AHA was to give thumbs-up to nutritious foods, it stupidly failed to anticipate the uproar that met the revelation that manufacturers had to pay as much as $640,000 *per brand per year* to win the AHA's approving nod. A later program, called On-Pack, met with greater success, though Michael Jacobson charged that the AHA's criteria were too lax. (Apparently several foods that taste tolerably good made the cut.)

Are Nutrient Supplements Nutritious?

Today one of the most hotly contested battles rages between the FDA and the nutrient supplement industry. More than 75 million Americans take such supplements, and even Michael Jacobson of the Center for Science in the Public Interest concedes, "Over the next ten years, supplements will be a very important part of nutrition."[44] In an astonishing admission, Jacobson says, "Sure you could have two or three carrots a day. But some people don't like carrots or prefer a pill."[45]

But don't be fooled into thinking that a common-sense virus has run riot through CSPI headquarters. The organization is steadfastly opposed to legislation that would liberate the supplement industry from stifling FDA regulation. We're not talking about permitting snake-oil salesmen to claim their little pills can make an impotent man virile overnight and grow hair on his bald head by dawn's first light. At issue is the right of a company to make truthful claims for its product.

"The FDA has had a historic bias against the dietary supplement industry,"[46] charges Gerald Kessler, who founded a supplement company called Nature's Plus. As Kessler notes, the FDA requires a company to prove its claims to the federal government's satisfaction: a process so onerous and expensive that few, if any, can afford it. So while medical researchers have found evidence that, say, vitamin E pills seem to reduce the risk of heart disease by 40 percent, sellers of such pills may not advertise this on their labels. The result is a knowledge deficiency and who knows how many preventable deaths? For as one anti-FDA group is fond of saying, "If a murderer kills you, it's homicide. If a drunk driver kills you, it's manslaughter. If the FDA kills you, it's just being cautious."[47]

Among the more creative nettles in the FDA's side have been Durk Pearson and Sandy Shaw, authors of the best-selling *Life Extension: A Practical Scientific Approach* (1982). Pearson and Shaw are great believers in nutrient supplements, and they chafe at their inability to get the word out. They write, "When we became interested in life extension in 1968, the limit on what you could do to extend your healthy active life span was information, because there was not much known about aging mechanisms. Now...the major limit on what you can do to extend your life span is regulatory barriers, especially those erected by the FDA."[48]

What particularly vexes them is the FDA's refusal to permit aspirin labels to impart information on the benefits of aspirin to those who have just suffered a heart attack. Several leading cardiologists, among them Charles H. Hennekens and Carl Pepine, editor of the *Journal of Myocardial Ischemia*, petitioned the FDA in 1992 to hurry up and approve the labeling petition filed by the Aspirin Foundation of America, Inc. The foundation requested FDA permission to add to professional aspirin labels (those directed at physicians) the phrase: "To reduce the risk of morbidity and mortality associated with acute heart attack, a dosage of 160 to 162.5 milligrams of aspirin (half a regular aspirin tablet) should be taken as soon as a heart attack is suspected and then daily for at least thirty days."[49]

The cardiologists noted that "routine use of at least 162 milligrams of aspirin therapy within twenty-four hours of an AMI (acute myocardial infarction, or heart attack) could save about 30,000 lives a year."[50]

But even if the FDA approves this professional label, why should potentially life-saving information be limited to physicians? Pearson and Shaw demand that the general aspirin-buying public be made privy as well, and their labors have included not only lawsuits but the puckish "First Amendment Aspirin Plus," marketed by the Life Extension Foundation as both a life-saver and an unauthorized middle finger flipped at FDA headquarters.

Nobel Laureate Milton Friedman has praised Pearson and Shaw's "split-label" proposal, by which "the manufacturer can make truthful health claims on the label; the FDA gets equal space and prominence on the label and can say what it wants."[51] Bending over backwards, Pearson and Shaw even suggest that products not approved by the FDA could have a modified *Ghostbusters* symbol—an FDA with a thick slash through it which is the visual equivalent of a rat poison warning. They have had no luck so far, but they, and a cluster of economists and consumer activists, continue to press radical reform on the obdurate FDA. Stay tuned.

Leading the congressional push for FDA reform is a rather improbable candidate: Senator Tom Harkin (D-Iowa) one of the last of the liberal Democrat true believers. But Senator Harkin has a maverick streak, and more importantly, he once had allergies, which he says were cured by bee pollen. "Something has got to be done to investigate into these things because it sure worked for me,"[52] he told a Senate hearing, and the something he has in mind he calls the Access to Medical Treatment Act, which would partially liberate practitioners of alternative medicine. (In 1990, the *New England Journal of Medicine* estimated that Americans spend almost $14 billion annually on alternative treatments: some quack, others effective.)

Harkin's bill would permit persons access to non-FDA approved treatments, as long as these treatments are not harmful (as bee pollen is not) and as long as the patients are counseled by a licensed practitioner that the therapy or product is not FDA-approved. So-called consumer groups protest, on the assumption that consumers are incapable of making their own decisions and the medical establishment is no more supportive. As Dr. Edward Campion wrote in the *New England Journal of Medicine*, alternative medicine is "in direct competition with conventional medicine. The public's expensive romance with unconventional medicine is reason for our profession to worry."[53]

But not to worry, Doctor: the timorous deregulators of the Republican Congress have yet to pass Harkin's bill, despite the cosponsorship of such influential Republican congressmen as Thomas DeLay (R-Tex.). For when it comes to ingesting food or drugs that may pose a risk, even if the benefits far outweigh such risk, nanny knows best.

6

Glow-in-the-Dark Eggs or Olestra: Pick Your Poison

> *Hypocrisy is the homage which vice*
> *pays to virtue.*
> —LaRochefoucauld, *Maxims,* 218

Let's say you swear by every minatory press release issued by CSPI and the entire thin-is-beautiful/I'll-have-the-low-fat-gruel-please dietary police. You haven't eaten Chinese since Mao Tse-Tung was riding herd. You regard Mexican food the way Ross Perot regards Mexicans. You spray-paint "Fettucini Alfredo = Death" on the sides of Italian restaurants. You even use your CSPI credit card when deciding to pig out on lentils.

When in January 1996 the Food and Drug Administration gave Procter and Gamble the thumbs-up to use olestra in savory snack foods (tortilla chips, crackers, potato chips, etc.) your first impulse may have been to shout Alleluia! This was the greatest invention since the CSPI-marketed "Vita-Mix Total Nutrition Center," the blender that guaranteed "no loss of the fiber-rich pulp"[1] and for only $445!

Olestra, you see, is the first no-fat, no-calorie, fat substitute. Made from sugar and vegetable oil, olestra's effect on the taste buds is that of an oil: it is pleasing, even aromatic. But its molecular bulk is six to eight fatty acids on its glycerol core, as opposed to three on the core of real fat, so that it has been dubbed "the stealth missile of fat molecules; it passes through the gastrointestinal tract without being digested or absorbed."[2] Its size prevents absorption. So you get the taste of fat without the avoirdupois. Moreover, unlike other fat substitutes, olestra remains stable at high temperatures, so it can achieve the impossible dream: a fat-free french fry that actually tastes like a french fry.

The health implications of a no-fat fat are revolutionary. Simply substituting olestra chips for regular potato chips can eliminate two-thirds of a person's excess fat intake. "It could literally save lives,"[3] as *Time* declared. Not to mention a pant size or two. For instance, a slice of peach pie contains 405 calories; made with olestra, it would contain 252. Olestra would reduce the caloric content of a piece of chocolate cake from 235 to 163. Comparable figures for other snacks include:

- Three chocolate-chip cookies: 138 calories today, 63 with olestra;
- One-half cup of chocolate ice cream: 270 calories today, 110 with olestra;
- One brownie: 85 calories today, 49 with olestra;
- One ounce of potato chips: 160 calories before olestra, 70 calories with olestra;

Olestra seems too good to be true. Unlike many low-fat foods, it possesses the taste of fat, so it's not an exercise in masochism to eat it. The consumer of an olestra chip may actually feel a twinge of pleasure—a new sensation for low-fat or no-fat dieters. For fat is essential to gastronomy. The American Dietetic Association has declared, "Fats are responsible for the texture, mouthfeel, and flavor of many foods, and make a major contribution to the palatability of the diet. Fats provide a variety of sought-after oral sensations, from crunchy to creamy, and help to make the diet flavorful, varied, and rich. Sensory preferences for fats are a characteristic human trait."[4] (What does this say about the humanness of the fat-phobes?)

A study conducted by researchers at Penn State University suggested that those who snack on olestra do not eat so voraciously as to cancel its benefits—a charge frequently made against low-fat foods. In the study, ninety-six "habitual snackers" were divided into two groups. One was fed olestra-prepared potato chips, the other group was given potato chips prepared with plain old frying oil. The olestra snackers knew that their chips were no-fat, and they consumed an average of 10 grams of chips more than the others yet they "ate on average 29 grams less fat and 270 fewer calories a day than those fed regular chips."[5] Truly this is the weight-conscious couch potato's fantasy come true.

Olestra's discovery was a typical case of serendipity scientists working late at the lab and all that monster mash stuff. Procter and Gamble scientists had been studying the difficulties that premature infants have in digesting fat; their tinkering led in 1968 to the invention of olestra, which is also known as a sucrose polyester. (You can understand why olestra is a better name than sucrose polyester, which conjures the image of a sugar daddy in a leisure suit.) Nineteen years of sweat and blood and taste tests later, Procter and Gamble filed a petition with the FDA. The company's original petition requested approval for olestra not just in snack foods but also for use in cooking oils; the cooking oils were dropped in 1990 when it became obvious that the entire South American rain forest would have to be felled to provide the paper necessary to print the studies that would sway the FDA.

As it was, Procter and Gamble supplied the FDA with more than 150,000 pages of data—more than 150 studies of pigs, dogs, and, in 98 cases, human beings making it "the most thoroughly tested new food ingredient ever considered by the FDA."[6] In the fall of 1990 the FDA's food advisory committee voted 15–5 to approve the P&G petition, with a couple of conditions attached. For one thing, manufacturers of olestra products (which P&G marketed under the name "Olean") must add vitamins A, D, E, and K, for the indications are that olestra, like real fat, absorbs these fat-soluble vitamins, but unlike real fat it takes them on the expressway right through the digestive system. This problem is solved easily enough: P&G simply adds enough A, D, E, and K to the olestra to sate the substance.

The body's absorption of carotenoids (the nutrients found in carrots and green leafy vegetables) is also inhibited by olestra, though as FDA chief David Kessler said when approving olestra, "the role of carotenoids in human health is not fully understood,"[7] and no remedial measures were prescribed. Indeed, carotenoid absorption is only a problem if you eat olestra and carotenoid-rich foods simultaneously, and we don't know many armchair chip-crunchers who pop cheese puffs with their right hand while unraveling a head of romaine lettuce with their left. Besides, b-carotene absorption is reduced almost as much by dietary soluble fibers as by olestra.

That, for P&G, was the easy part. Sure, the folks at the Center for Science in the Public Interest complained that "even though there is no absolute proof that carotenoids *prevent* disease, it's foolhardy to add something to the food supply that steals them from the body."[8] Here, on the olestra battlefield, was CSPI in all its nerd-tyrannical glory. It wasn't issuing the usual ultracautious advice to the perpetually frightened. No, CSPI was demanding that the FDA keep olestra *off* the market: CSPI was fighting to limit the dietary choices available to the American people. It's one thing to weigh in on the question of whether or not a snacker should trade carotenoids for fat; it's another thing altogether to deprive her of that choice.

Fecal Urgency and Other Issues

There was one other FDA string attached, and a helluva string it was. Products made from olestra must bear this label: "This Product Contains Olestra. Olestra may cause abdominal cramping and loose stools. Olestra inhibits the absorption of some vitamins and other nutrients. Vitamins A, D, E, and K have been added."

That second sentence is, shall we say, a disincentive to appetite. And it illuminates health nannyism at its most sensational, not to mention scatological.

Diarrhea is an unpleasant, if fairly rare, side effect experienced by a tiny percentage of olestra eaters. Fred Mattson, an emeritus professor at the University of California at San Diego and part of Procter and Gamble's original olestra research team, remembers, "We had a great deal of trouble with what we called anal leakage."[9] Olestra just, well, slid through the body. Not a pretty picture, though P&G scientists came to the rescue by increasing the viscosity of the substance's molecular structure.

Among the mounds of data submitted to the FDA were tests indicating that olestra's effect on the gastrointestinal system was negligible even for those suffering from ulcerative colitis and Crohn's disease. In one study, 3,357 people snacked on either olestra-based munchies or conventional snacks for a five-month period. Although some minor differences were reported—olestra was more frequently associated with flatulence, conventional snacks with belching (take your pick)—there was "no statistically significantly difference"[10] in reporting any of these symptoms: loose stool, diarrhea, passing gas, abdominal cramp, heartburn, nausea, bloating, constipation, urgent bowel movement, and belching. Reams of paper were submitted to the FDA covering olestra's effect on such dinner-table discussion topics as stool consistency and passage of oil from the rectum. Perhaps the most memorable moment of the FDA meeting in the fall of 1995 came when the Procter and Gamble medical director told the panel that P&G had asked more than 1,000 human guinea pigs "with photographic prompts, whether they experienced any oily staining of their underwear."[11] One picture worth a thousand words, indeed.

Several gastroenterologists testified to olestra's harmlessness before the FDA panel. The consensus was that for some people, olestra could have the same temporary effects as does a switch from a low-fiber to a high-fiber diet. As an FDA press release admitted, "These gastrointestinal effects do not have medical consequences."[12]

Michael Pariza, director of the Food Research Institute at the University of Wisconsin-Madison, told Consumer Alert that olestra "is less of a problem than baked beans, dietary fiber, or prunes...even honey."[13] Indeed, as Consumer Alert's John Berlau notes, the National Institutes of Health has warned that one food ingredient causes "nausea, cramps, bloating, gas, and diarrhea"[14] in up to 20 percent of Americans. No, it's not olestra, but rather the lactose in milk. Which remains on supermarket shelves, at least for now.

The Publicity Machine

When Procter and Gamble announced that Max chips, made from olestra, would be test-marketed in three small cities, Michael Jacobson sprang into action (which, as always, happened to be a press conference at the National Press Club with television cameras present). Grand Junction, Colorado; Cedar Rapids, Iowa; and Eau Claire, Wisconsin—the three test markets—were dubbed the "diarrhea capitals"[15] of America by CSPI. Jacobson introduced three chip eaters who had suffered various indignities allegedly visited upon them by Max chips, and he helpfully included printed "case histories" of almost twenty ailing chip-eaters in the Grand Junction, Cedar Rapids, and Eau Claire environs. Reporters laughed out loud as Jacobson related such "heartbreaking" tales as these:

- "A seventy-eight-year-old lawyer in Cedar Rapids ate an ounce of chips with dinner. At 3:30 A.M. he woke up with fecal urgency, but he couldn't get to the bathroom in time."[16]
- "A woman told a Wisconsin radio station that her healthy, eighty-three-year-old mother ate some Max chips and couldn't leave the house for three days while she shuttled back and forth from the bedroom to the bathroom."[17]
- "A sixty-five-year-old homemaker in Grand Junction who nibbled from a bag of chips experienced extreme fecal urgency, and did not make it to the bathroom in time."[18]

These "gastrointestinal horror stories" were only a foretaste of our feculent future, warned Jacobson. "It is only a matter of time before products containing olestra cause deaths,"[19] he asserted wildly, citing "driving" as a potentially risky activity for those experiencing catastrophic anal leakage.

The Center put on its gawky white-guy version of the full-court press. A toll-free CSPI phone number for olestra complaints was created; more than 192 people who had eaten Max chips and suffered registered complaints. A CSPI-commissioned poll found that 20 percent of the respondents had "experienced cramps, loose stools, diarrhea, or other adverse effects"[20] from eating Max chips.

"The media dutifully reported the study," noted Stephen Glass, without talking to gastroenterologists, who dispute these types of reports. Physicians say that it is clinically difficult, if not impossible, for people to link diarrhea with any specific food, especially after eating it only once. Plus, the survey was far from a model poll. CSPI's earlier advertisements may have already conditioned the respondents negatively toward the chips."[21] The poll itself was a joke: Harry W. O'Neill of Roper Marketing and Public Opinion Research detailed its numerous flaws, among them biased questions, improper interviewing method, and small sample.

But the damage was done. Millions of Americans now associate diarrhea with a product that once held out the promise of creating fat-free snacks. A typical book on the shelf in the diet section at Border's states, "experts argue that there are no assurances that this controversial, indigestible fat substitute won't ultimately pose a significant danger to your health."[22] And who, you ask, are these "experts"? Why, the authors note, none other than those famously dispassionate seekers of the truth...the Center for Science in the Public Interest.

If CSPI intended to smear olestra, it succeeded. Some in the mainstream media tried to report the story fairly: *Time* created a taste-test panel to consume the notorious chips, and it found that "the chips taste like chips. Not bad chips (each of us takes another) but not jim-dandy chips, either. Mouth feel...is about right.... Finger feel is pretty good, too. Pick up a chip and your thumb and forefinger get greasy, just as nature intended. But there is an aftertaste...not really unpleasant."[23]

Ho-hum. *This* is the product that will bring down Western civilization?

Only the most sobersided prude could read the CSPI attack on olestra without emitting a few adolescent snorts. The fat-substitute is damned as "a great propagator of catastrophic anal leakage."[24] (Put *that* on the label and watch the bags of chips glue themselves to the shelf.) "Greasy feces" and underwear stains are said to be among the perils awaiting the Max eater. Song parodies were sung: "Say it loud when there's painful bloating/Say it soft when your sphincter's floating."[25] Few people this side of a three-year old or a Jim Carrey movie have ever gotten so much mileage from the comic potential of the potty. Let's face it: The CSPI campaign ruined olestra-based products as "date" snacks. Not even the bravest sixteen-year-old boy or girl wants to go to the movies with a date after eating Max chips. The embarrassment potential boggles the teenage mind. Fecal urgency is not a classic turn-on.

The Center for Science in the Public Interest smears people as carelessly as some of us step on ants. *Nutrition Action Healthletter* derided the "paid consultants that P&G has trotted out to defend its $280 million gamble."[26] This is a cheap and cowardly ploy: attacking the scientists (many of whom were *not* paid P&G consultants) instead of their work. Not that they didn't cast aspersions upon the work as well, but these aspersions vanished into thin air once challenged.

David Allison, a Columbia University scientist and member of the FDA's food advisory panel, told Stephen Glass of the *New Republic* that CSPI's denigration of olestra research was a joke. "I ran a quick and dirty calculation and found [that CSPI's claim] wasn't the case. When I questioned them, they said they didn't do a formal statistical analysis, they just eyeballed the data. In my opinion, that's behaving inappropriately…their statements implied and were intended to imply they had conducted analysis which they hadn't."[27]

The countless eminences of the scientific and medical worlds who weighed in on behalf of olestra could not erase the image of fecal urgency. Dr. Louis Sullivan, former Secretary of Health and Human Services and president of Morehouse School of Medicine, told the *New York Times* that "all Americans can feel confident in the safety of snacks made with olestra."[28] Professors, deans, and directors from such institutions as the University of Washington, Tufts University, George Washington University, and the American Health Foundation publicly endorsed Olean, the name P&G gave olestra. But it's hard to dissolve a slander.

Why the anti-olestra hysteria? Is it simply because CSPI cares less about promoting health than discouraging enjoyment? Must we all wear the hair shirt? Is the problem not the fat in the chip but the chip itself? Does the chip symbolize life, freedom, enjoyment? What drives people to write, as CSPI staffers did in *Nutrition Action Healthletter*, "olestra's tendency to wreak havoc on your gut may be the best thing about it…if it discourages would-be eaters"?[29] What kinds of people wish abdominal cramping and diarrhea on those who choose a different diet? Whatever flatulence the odd Max chip may cause is nothing compared to the gaseous honk from the Center for Science in the Public Interest.

Stephen Glass caught Jacobson in all his loony hyper-paternalism. The CSPI honcho suggested that the FDA require, at the very *mini-*

mum, this warning label: "Olestra may cause diarrhea, loose stools, increased bowel movements, fecal urgency, gas and cramps. Symptoms may be severe and persistent. Olestra can cause yellow-orange underwear staining, greasy bowel movements, and yellow-orange discoloration of your stool."

Glass writes:

> I asked Jacobson if there was any condition under which it would be okay for P&G to sell the chips to adults. What if we had his ideal label on the package one that says these chips could kill you—would that be okay?
>
> "No. It might be hard to see on the back of the bag," he said.
>
> Okay. So what if we put it on the front of the bag?
>
> "People still might not see it. It could get scrunched down."
>
> Let's say we put it in a cardboard box that can't fold up.
>
> "They still might not read it before they ate the chips."
>
> What if we put blinking lights around it?
>
> "No. Let's say you're at a party and they're mixed in a bowl with regular chips, how will you know?"
>
> What if we required them to dye the chips blue?
>
> "I don't think so," he insisted. "I mean, I don't know, say the consumer was blind...."[30]

Thanks in large part to this neurotic, millions of Americans who crave chips but really ought to lose a few pounds are faced with an either-or proposition. Choice is the loser. And so is health. Just who, Mr. Jacobson, wins?

Three Cheers for Food Poisoning!

Okay, so our fussy Washington nannies don't want us to eat olestra-based products. Accept, for a moment, that if you tell yourself enough lurid tales of fecal urgency then eventually you'll live in mortal fear of stained underwear, and you'll want to save other complete strangers from this fate worse than death. We all have our blind spots, our irrational hatreds: might the campaign against olestra be anomalous?

Of course not. For CSPI and its crew of fussbudgets, along with a truth-averse group known as Food & Water, Inc. have also waged a hysterical campaign against the irradiation of food—a process that promises to make our poultry, vegetables, fish, and even red meat safer than we had ever imagined possible.

Recall the widespread panic in 1993, when three persons died and hundreds of others were taken seriously ill by an outbreak of *E. coli* 0157:H7 in the Pacific Northwest. The etiology of the outbreak was frighteningly commonplace: it all appeared to stem from undercooked bacteria-tainted hamburgers sold at a few outlets in the Jack-in-the-Box chain. Death by take-out burger: it sounded like a Stephen King novel. If only.

And the death-in-the-box scare was not an isolated occurrence. As many as 500 Americans die each year as the result of an *E. coli* infection; up to 20,000 more are taken ill by the ingestion of these bacteria, which is found in the intestines and feces of cows. (We do hope you're not reading this on a lunch break, hand grasping a burger.)

An understandable panic erupted; Jack-in-the-Box sales fell, not surprisingly, and backyard burger-flippers in their "Kiss the Chef" aprons burned patties beyond recognition. But there is an alternative to resigning oneself to a lifetime of charred pitch-black hamburgers—an alternative that, had it been in use in 1993, almost certainly would have prevented the *E. coli* outbreak and saved those lives. The alternative is irradiation.

You probably felt a twinge when you read the word "irradiation." We've all seen the 1950s science-fiction movies in which scaly under-sea creatures or oversized insects, the mutant consequences of radiation, destroy Tokyo or Main Street, USA. Sure, you might think, radiation will kill the *E. coli* and give us giant mutant hamburgers that prefer their humans with a dash of ketchup!

Thankfully, the radiation that so many scientists regard as the surest way to prevent food-borne disease is rather less virulent. It is both simple and remarkably effective. The food, which can be packaged individually or in bulk, is exposed to a modest dose of gamma rays, machine-generated electrons, or X-rays. (Dosage for poultry, for example, is 1.5 to 3.0 kilorays.) The energy passes through the food, leaving no residue, and it destroys bacteria, molds, yeasts, and insects. Countless studies have demonstrated that irradiation wipes out from 99.5 to 99.9 percent of such bacteria and parasites as *salmonella*, *E. coli*, *Listeria monocytegenes Campylobacter*, the *Virbios*, and *Trichinella spiralis*.

We're not talking merely about nuisance bacteria of the sort that give you an upset stomach for the night. The Centers for Disease Control estimates that these microorganisms and parasites are responsible for 10,000 deaths annually in the United States and between 24 million and 81 million cases of CSPI's favorite malady, diarrhea. Yearly economic losses are set at between $7.7 and $23 billion. The damage done overseas, particularly in the Third World, is little short of catastrophic. A joint FAO (Food and Agriculture Organization of the United Nations)-World Health Organization Expert Committee on Food Safety found that "illness due to contaminated food is perhaps the most widespread health problem in the contemporary world."[31] About one-quarter of all deaths in developing countries are due to diarrhea; up to 70 percent of these cases of diarrhea are traceable to food-borne agents.

So the public health implications of irradiation are staggering. (Ask an African who is hosting a five-foot long tapeworm what he thinks of irradiation.) Dr. Douglas Archer, Deputy Director of the FDA's Center for Food Safety and Applied Nutrition, avers, "If poultry irradiation were widely used in this country, I believe it could prevent hundreds of thousands of illnesses and hundreds of deaths ever year."[32] As for *E. coli* 0157:H7, a panel of the American Gastroenterological Association Foundation stated that this bacteria's elimination "is currently impossible unless the product is thoroughly cooked or irradiated."[33]

On top of the lives saved and illnesses prevented, irradiation's promise can be measured in dollars and cents. It extends the shelf life of fruits and vegetables: by three weeks for strawberries, tomatoes, and mushrooms. This is a tremendous potential boon to Third World people. Countries (including the United States) have increasingly banned the importation of agricultural products treated with chemical insecticides; irradiation is both more effective than these fumigants and certainly far less of a hazard. Export markets beckon, not only for fruits and vegetables but also for more exotic products such as frog legs and spices.

Irradiation does to solids what pasteurization does to liquids. But the similarities do not end there. Both processes have inspired feverish if uninformed opposition. Observes Dr. Fritz Käferstein, chief of the Food Safety Unit of the World Health Organization, "this ongoing campaign for public acceptance of food irradiation is a carbon copy of the story of pasteurization, the process which is taken for granted today by everyone. Attempts to introduce it as a general public health practice at the turn of the century were successfully stonewalled by using similar arguments as employed by opponents of food irradiation: It will be used to clean up unacceptably contaminated food, the food will become dead, the list goes on and on. Scientific research, however, shows that this is a perfectly sound food preservation technology badly needed in a world where food-borne diseases are on the increase and where between one-quarter and one-third of the global food supply is lost post-harvest."[34]

More than half of many agricultural products are lost post-harvest in Africa: imagine the bounty that irradiation could provide. But it has not yet, and the ignorant calumnies heaped upon irradiation may retard its acceptance for years to come. As food-safety Professor Mark Tamplin of the University of Florida observes, public resistance is "a knee-jerk reaction that happens when you combine the word 'food' with the word 'radiation.'"[35]

The U.S. government approved irradiation of poultry, fruits, vegetables, pork, flour, and spices years ago, and finally approved the irradiation of red meat in December of 1997—after several dozen people died from *E. coli* poisoning over the summer. In this instance, government is no longer the roadblock; it's the professional fraidy cats at Food & Water and the silly hysterics at CSPI.

The largest domestic market for irradiated chicken is hospitals and nursing homes which are not exactly known for flamboyant and devil-may-care cuisine. One would think that chicken fed to ninety-year-old invalids would be safe enough even for Michael Jacobson, but no. Astronauts are also connoisseurs of the irradiated, particularly steak and turkey, though their endorsement track record (Tang) does not inspire much confidence in the supermarket future of smoked turkey à la cobalt.

But the supper of astronauts has been praised by none other than Julia Child, the culinary doyenne of America, the woman who taught America to cook, as she is often called. Ms. Child dismisses the alarmists: "Irradiation of food is all right, too. A lot of Nervous Nellies are afraid of it, but there's absolutely no scientific proof that any radiation stays in the food. It just kills all the bacteria and makes the food safer. Anything is a good idea if it can keep people from getting sick."[36]

Irradiation seems not to leave an aftertaste (though a small minority of those who have eaten the products dissent). Early reports from those brave enough to stock irradiated products and invite the hoots and catcalls and pickets of Food & Water have been auspicious. The first Midwestern store to stock irradiated strawberries and citrus fruits, Carrot Top of Northbrook, Illinois, has done a land-office business. As owner Jim Corrigan says, "By stocking irradiated produce, I can reduce my retail price because there is less spoilage...and my customers can enjoy the benefits of increased shelf life."[37] The loss of nutritional value incurred by irradiated products is no different from that experienced by those that are conventionally processed. Fresh is best, as always, but if fresh is unavailable, irradiated foods are a respectable second.

In any event, the nutrient loss is negligible. Researchers have found that "even if all of the pork in the United States were to be irradiated, only 2.3 percent of vitamin B1 in the diet of Americans would be lost."[38] Irradiated foods are usually somewhat pricier than others: chicken, for instance, would probably cost a dime a pound more were the irradiated fowl to show up on supermarket shelves.

Not that it will show up anytime soon. No supermarket chains are willing to take the plunge, which means that Sal Manella may still be hanging around the local butcher's block. Forty countries have embraced the zapping of food to cleanse it of bacteria, and even those government agencies and health organizations susceptible to pressure from the Chicken Littles have approved the use of food irradiation: the Food and Drug Administration, the U.S. Department of Agriculture, the American Medical Association, the Mayo Clinic, the World Health Organization, and the United Nations Food and Agriculture Organization. (The U.S. government requires packages of irradiated poultry to be decorated with the florid "radura," the creepy green international symbol for radiation, as well as a label reading either "Treated with Radiation" or "Treated by Irradiation." Those who have lived through the nuclear age can not help but be made a bit queasy by such symbols, even though irradiation no more makes your chicken radioactive than passing your suitcase along an airport security belt makes your luggage radioactive. Old fears die hard.)

Evidently glow-in-the-dark suitcases are a commonplace at Food & Water, headquarters of the anti-irradiation zealots. Food & Water is the progeny of a New Jersey osteopath named Walter Burnstein. Like all such pressure groups, it needs a devil to focus the attention (and loosen the pursestrings) of its members. For years, Teddy Kennedy played Great Satan for the conservatives and Jesse Helms did the honors when liberals wanted to raise a buck or two. To Food & Water, irradiation is Ted and Jesse rolled into one, with Hillary Clinton and Newt Gingrich tossed in for good measure.

A typical Food & Water ad includes the underlined claim that "studies have demonstrated that consuming food exposed to radiation may pose serious cancer risks."[39] That is a powerful line, but there is just one itty bitty problem: there are no such studies.

Food & Water was exposed as a band of ignorant dilettantes in one of investigative television's finest hours. John Stossel, correspondent for ABC-television's news magazine *20/20*, reported on the unsuccessful Food & Water-coordinated protest to keep Vindicator from opening the nation's first commercial food irradiation plant in Mulberry, Florida.

Anti-Vindicator protesters had marched carrying such signs as "Hell No, We Won't Glow," but perhaps a more fitting sign would have read, "Hell No, We Don't Know." For John Stossel's report revealed an anti-irradiation movement utterly bereft of knowledge and scruples.

"They play loose with facts," noted Stossel in his televised skewering. The report was a classic. A boyish dimwit named Michael Colby was the telegenic face of Food & Water, and his inability to respond to Stossel's questions was painful to behold.

Colby burbled, "If you look at the existing studies on humans and animals fed irradiated food, you will find testicular tumors, chromosomal abnormalities, kidney damage, and cancer and birth defects."

"Caused because somebody ate irradiated food?" asked an incredulous Stossel.

"Absolutely. Absolutely," replied Colby.

At which point Stossel told Colby that he had talked to the author of the study Colby cited, and she had told Stossel that she "never said the kids were developing cancer."

To which Colby replied...well, what could he say? He had been caught in a...shall we say "exaggeration," and Food & Water had to lick its embarrassing wounds and live, alas, to fight another day.[40]

During the anti-Vindicator fight, Food & Water ran a radio ad containing this memorable threat: "What if you found out that those fresh fruits and vegetables everyone keeps telling you to eat more of...might kill you?"[41]

A catchy hook, to be sure. The ad continued, "many scientists are saying irradiation makes foods unsafe...and new studies show that ingesting radiation-exposed foods causes genetic damage, which can lead to cancer, and birth defects."[42]

The ad was designed by the legendary Tony Schwartz, the "guerilla media" guru who designed the infamous 1964 television ad which showed a young girl picking daisy petals as the announcer counts "Ten, nine, eight," and so on, all the way down to nuclear Armageddon. The implication was that Senator Barry Goldwater, if elected President, would nuke poor Susie and kill all the flowers. So instead we elected President Lyndon Johnson, the well-known man of peace. The daisy ad is still regarded as the single most brutal television ad ever shown in this country.

Yet Tony Schwartz, obviously no shrinking violet, disavowed the ad he did for Food & Water. "I'm retracting my support for the ad,"[43] he told the *Wall Street Journal*, noting that it was factually incorrect. He used stronger language in an interview with John Stossel on that same

20/20 program. Schwartz told the ABC reporter that Food & Water had behaved in a "sleazy" manner and when a former hatchet man for Lyndon Johnson calls you sleazy, you are *sleazy*.

The Stossel piece may have humiliated Food & Water, but they haven't gone away. They're still plugging: one day sending a snotty letter to companies that express a willingness to consider selling irradiated products ("Please trust that the last thing Food & Water wants to do is begin a national grassroots effort directed at your fine corporation,"[44] pouts one Colby missive); the next day demanding that the government pump more money into methods of meat inspection that are not as effective as irradiation.

Both Food & Water and CSPI demand an infusion of taxpayer dollars to combat E. coli and other food-borne diseases, but there is absolutely no reason to believe that hiring a few hundred (or thousand, or hundreds of thousands) more meat inspectors will make one bit of difference in the healthfulness of the 117 million animal carcasses these inspectors examine each year. As former Assistant Attorney General James Steele, a professor emeritus at the University of Texas School of Public Health, has written, "*E. coli* 0157:H7 is not known to cause any diseases with clinical signs in cattle. Cattle are passive carriers of this virulent form of colon bacteria and there is no way the Federal inspectors can identify a carrier animal by physical examination. This problem is not limited to examination for *E. coli* but is the same for determining what animals and poultry may be the carriers of *Salmonella, Campylobacter, Listeria monocytogenes,* and *Yersinia.* The presence of these pathogens in raw meat is undesirable but unavoidable."[45]

Irradiation, the best hope for destroying these pathogens, has yet to gain widespread acceptance, in large part because of the actions of Food & Water and its brethren in hysteria. There is reason for hope, however. Dr. Christine Bruhn of the University of California-Davis has said, "The activists may not want irradiated food, but they're simply wrong in claiming the public opposes it, too,"[46] and there is reason to believe her. A Gallup poll of 1993 found that only 24 percent of respondents knew anything about food irradiation. Once its benefits were explained, 54 percent said they would be more likely to purchase irradiated than non-irradiated meat, and in what might be called the Jack-in-the-Box syndrome, a full 60 percent said they would pay a five percent premium for irradiated hamburger.[47]

Dr. Allan Forbes, former director of the FDA Office of Nutrition and Food Sciences, says of Food & Water and the other "public-interest" magpies: "They've lost sight of what the public interest is. Food irradiation is safe beyond the slightest question. It's a sad commentary, but it's clear to me that these groups make their living by creating fear about issues like this."[48]

Should We Worry about Giant Cow Disease?

If the threat of Kentucky-fried isotopes isn't severe enough, how about the impending danger of an outbreak of acromelagy, whose symptoms include the enlargement of the chin? Imagine a planet of Jay Lenos! Without the gag writers. If you can, then you're just the kind of sucker to fall for the scare stories engineered by the critics of bovine growth hormone (BGH).

BGH, also known, technically, as BST (bovine somatropin), has been tested and retested for more than six decades; it may turn out to be one of the best friends low-income consumers have ever had. For dairy farmers, too—BGH has been called "the biggest thing to hit American dairying since artificial insemination."[49] Manufactured by a process similar to that used to create synthetic human insulin, BGH is a protein hormone injected into the rump of lactating cows. In no way does BGH alter the genetic makeup of the cow. Indeed, BST occurs naturally in cows, and is present in milk from cows that have never received an injection of the growth hormone. By taste, appearance, and nutritional value, BGH milk is no different from non-BGH milk.

BGH greatly increases a cow's milk production. The boost is anywhere between 10 and 25 percent. In a market economy, you might expect that an explosive increase in milk production would bring down milk prices, which would be a blessing especially to the people on the bottom of the economic pile: young single mothers of small milk-drinking children. But the entangling network of price supports, quotas, and subsidies that frames our agricultural economy is to the market what the extemporaneous speeches of George Bush were to classic oratory. As a result, BGH is trapped in a political no-man's land whose terrain we shall map out presently.

After the usual exhaustive and frightfully expensive studies, the FDA approved use of BGH on dairy cattle in 1993 and refused to require any sort of labeling, as there is no real difference between milk from BGH-treated kine and milk from your average cud-chewer. The FDA "concluded that BST has no appreciable effect on the composition of milk produced by treated cows and that there are no human safety or health concerns associated with food products derived from cows treated with BST."[50]

But if you think that's the end of the story, and we all drank oceans of milk happily ever after, you haven't been reading this book very carefully. For the usual suspects took their places on the field, and the game began.

Food & Water blared, "BGH is a dangerous, genetically engineered hormone that poses serious health hazards to both cows and humans."[51] A rather more formidable, less buffoonish outfit, the Washington, DC-based Foundation on Economic Trends, led by biotechnology's arch-enemy, Jeremy Rifkin, registered as its "primary concerns" that "the drug has major health impacts on cows; *will cost tens of thousands of dairy farmers their jobs* (because it will create a milk-surplus crisis); and has unknown, but feared, effects on human consumers."[52] The attacks were too much for biotechnology analyst Stuart Weisbrod, who called the critics "flat-Earthers. They're looking at all the evidence and refusing to believe it."[53]

The flat-Earth society platform was spelled out most vividly in a 1994 article in *Harper's Magazine* by Tony Hiss, who remembering his rustic summers in Peacham, Vermont, as a privileged youth, returned to the Green Mountain State and admitted that "it requires some serious squinting to re-create the old picture-postcard views that I remember so well from the Forties and Fifties."[54] Hiss bemoans the decline of the dairy-farm culture in Vermont, which has lost one farm a week in recent years and is down to about 2,000 such farms. No question: this has taken a toll on Vermont, aesthetically and culturally, though the culprit has not been BST but rather a federal agricultural policy that both shackles and subsidizes farmers and that told our patrons of husbandry to "get big or get out" all through the 1970s, thus encouraging serious overextension throughout the industry.

Hiss scrounged up the handful of BGH critics for his story. It seems that a University of Vermont veterinarian named Dr. Marla Lyng "observed several dozen Holstein cows that had undergone BGH testing in a clinical trial sponsored by Monsanto."[55] Lyng told Rural Vermont, an advocacy organization, that several of the cows seemed to have mastitis, an udder infection characterized by pus; some also had open wounds on their hind legs. Rural Vermont used Lyng's observations to produce a report that warned, "While definitive conclusions cannot be drawn to prove that BGH is a definite health hazard for dairy animals, there seem to be many reasons for concern."[56]

The infections allegedly common in BGH cows are usually treated by antibiotics: the threat of these antibiotics being passed on to the humans who drink milk from the mending cows "raises questions not only of animal safety but of human health as well,"[57] declared Rural Vermont.

The report was big news in Vermont. Monsanto spokesmen dismissed it as unscientific, which was to be expected, but the FDA soon weighed in, on Monsanto's side. FDA Associate Commissioner Marc Scheineson told Senator Patrick Leahy (D-Vt.) that of the fifty-six cows listed by Rural Vermont as being BGH-treated, "at least nine were *untreated control* cows."[58] Such a whopper of a mistake renders the Rural Vermont report worthless. A 1993 study of 1.7 million tankers of milk found that only 0.07 percent of the sample exceeded the FDA limit on antibiotic residues, and of course that milk was immediately disposed of.

Numerous other researchers contradicted Rural Vermont's claims. On the matter of pus (not exactly an appetizing prospect), the *Journal of Dairy Science* "found a decreased risk of udder infection for every thousand quarts of milk produced by BST-treated cows."[59]

In a definitive study in the *Journal of the American Medical Association*, William H. Daughaday, MD, of the Department of Internal Medicine of the Washington University School of Medicine and David M. Barbano, Ph.D., of Cornell University's Department of Food Science, found BGH to be completely safe and wholesome. Bovine somatropin is usually present in milk from unsupplemented cows, they noted, and besides, "it has no biological effect on humans for two reasons: when ingested...[it is] broken down by digestive enzymes into amino acids and small peptides, as is any other protein in the diet; and even if BST did enter the body in substantial amounts, it is *not* biologically active."[60]

In any event, the scare stories are a smokescreen: as the United States Court of Appeals for the Second Circuit noted in striking down a Vermont BGH-labeling law, "It is undisputed that the dairy products derived from herds treated with BGH are indistinguishable from products derived from untreated herds."[61]

The real concern of the anti-BGH crusaders is not cow mastitis but the agricultural economy. They fear, as Tony Hiss writes, that BGH may "drive hundreds more Vermonters out of business."[62] Hiss sees the salvation of dairy farmers in higher prices; thus, his opposition to BGH. "The number of active milk farms in Vermont could well double over the next ten years if the price farmers get for their milk were allowed to increase by as little as 15 percent."[63]

Consumers, particularly the poor, who spend a disproportionate percentage of their income on staples such as milk, may look at this with a rather more jaundiced eye. Dr. Charles Grossman, in an editorial in the *Journal of the American Medical Association*, cut to the marrow:

> Clearly, the increased milk production coupled with a more efficient use of feed by the dairy cows will result in economic gains for the farmer. However, because milk prices are regulated by a governmental price-support program, introduction of bovine somatropin could increase milk supplies, necessitating either a reduction in the support price or restriction in production. This would eventually lead to fewer cows on existing farms or fewer farms in the nation. Those farmers, however, who adopt the use of this hormone early on and who have superior managerial skills will be successful.[64]

James Bovard, author of *Farm Fiasco* and a respected critic of the U.S. agriculture program, has called BGH "the silver bullet to kill the dairy program."[65] As Consumer Alert's Jon Berlau explains, "With BGH, milk yields will increase so much that the increased costs of subsidizing milk will pressure the government to either lower the supports or do away with them altogether. Either way, the consumer wins because milk prices go down."[66] Besides, because of all the government subsidies, there are too many dairy farmers whose primary goal is to milk the taxpayers.

And this is the crux of the matter: should the U.S. government continue to subsidize the production of milk, which, thanks to BGH, will flow more freely (and cheaply) than ever before? This is a political question, not a scientific question but the cause of expensive milk is so difficult to defend that one almost can't blame Rural Vermont and the others for their sleight of hand.

The *Journal of the American Medical Association* declared that "it is both inappropriate and wrong for special-interest groups to play on the health and safety fears of the public to further their own ends."[67] Even C. Everett Koop, the former Surgeon General not known for his *laissez-faire* bent, called the attacks on BGH "baseless, manipulative, and irresponsible."[68]

But as long as they keep the coffers filled, and make the direct mail packages ever sexier, the attacks won't stop at least until the nannies sniff out more lucrative doomsday products to wail about.

Before we leave the cows to their lactating, we should note that Jeremy Rifkin, though he made mention of the loss of jobs in his brief against BGH, had noneconomic reasons for his position. Rifkin's real fear is of biotechnology. BGH, which is manufactured by Monsanto

Company, Eli Lilly and Company, Upjohn Company, and American Cyanamid Company, is poised to become "biotechnology's first big blockbuster project,"[69] and Rifkin is biotech's sworn enemy, its most uncompromising foe. And as we shall learn in the next chapter, Rifkin sees the world in such starkly black and white hues that he makes your average cow look gray.

7

What's Jeremy Rifkin's Beef?: The War on Our Not-So-Sacred Cow

> "**Lud·dite** (ludīt), n. **1.** a member of any
> various bands of workers in England (1811–
> 1816) who destroyed industrial machinery in
> the belief that its use diminished employment.
> **2.** any opponent of new technologies or
> technological change."
> —*Webster's College Dictionary*

If Jeremy Rifkin did not exist, it would not be necessary to invent him, as he seems constitutionally opposed to invention of any sort.

A balding, mustachioed man who looks like a mild-mannered assistant professor, Rifkin has become the scourge of biotechnology, the sworn enemy of the cow, and, just maybe—if you suffer from sickle-cell anemia, colorectal cancer, AIDS, or any of a hundred other fatal diseases—the most dangerous man in America.

Jeremy Rifkin was a moderately successful 1960s protester: he didn't strike it rich and marry a movie star, like Tom Hayden did, but he made a headline now and then. He graduated in 1967 from the Wharton School of Finance, of all places, and also took a master's degree in international affairs from the Fletcher School of Law and Diplomacy at Tufts University. Rifkin's first real prominence came as head of the Peoples Bicentennial Commission, a run-of-the-mill leftist group which tried, and failed, to steer the nation's bicentennial observance in a collectivist direction. Rifkin's goal, as he wrote in 1973, was to create a society in which "Human rights are placed above property values; Personal interests can be identified with the collective interest; Health care is a human right rather than a marketplace commodity going to the highest bidder; Technology is made to serve rather than to exploit man and the environment."[1] Fairly standard socialist boilerplate, and had he kept at it from this angle Rifkin would have faded into the obscurity that swallowed his fellow travelers.

But in the mid-1970s, after the Peoples Bicentennial Commission disappeared, to the apparent indifference of the People, Jeremy Rifkin found a new cause. A sexy cause. A lucrative cause. (At least to judge from his recent purchase of a nearly half-million dollar home in one of Washington, DC's fashionable neighborhoods.) That cause: screeching, hysterical opposition to biotechnology.

Jeremy Rifkin shares Michael Jacobson's hunger for publicity, but whereas Jacobson and CSPI exhibit occasional wit and creativity, Rifkin prefers the blunt and relentless approach. He seized leadership of the nascent anti-biotech movement in 1977, when he and a band of protesters interrupted a meeting of molecular biologists at the National Academy of Sciences. As one participant recalled, "They jumped up singing, 'We shall not be cloned.' Then they unfurled banners and linked them all around the room. We were their hostages. We were being terrorized."[2]

They were also being travestied. No responsible scientist advocates human cloning; that is certainly *not* what biotechnology is about. But by shifting the focus from biotech's potential to create disease-resistant plants or even a cure for cancer to such outrageous improbabilities as human cloning or eugenics, Rifkin has succeeded in planting the seed of doubt in millions of minds. No matter that reputable researchers regard him as a charlatan. Paleontologist Stephen Jay Gould trashed one Rifkin book on biotech as "a cleverly constructed tract of anti-intellectual propaganda masquerading as scholarship. Among books promoted as serious intellectual statements by important thinkers, I don't think I have ever read a shoddier work.... [It] belongs in the sordid company of anti-science."[3]

And Gould's was a virtual valentine in the world of Rifkin reviews. Monsanto's Jerry Caulder, who owns a doctorate in agronomy and plant physiology, charges that "Rifkin is an absolute master at confusing the possible with the probable. If someone were to ask me whether it's possible for a spaceship to descend in my parking lot and for aliens to communicate with me, I would have to say that it is. But if you ask me if it's probable, I'm sure as hell not going to wait for them to show up at lunch tomorrow. That's the difference between possible and probable, and why scientists find it difficult defending themselves against Rifkin's antitechnology fanaticism."[4]

The problem, as the eminent ethicist Arthur L. Caplan says, is the word "gene." For "there is plain irrational fear. I call it genophobia. Genoneurosis. Gene psychosis. You say 'gene' and people lose their ethical bearings. They immediately assume that the clone of Adolph Hitler is coming over the hill."[5]

Not that scientists haven't worried about the very same thing. From 1973–75, men and women of science observed a two-year moratorium on recombinant-DNA experiments while the promises, dangers, risks, and ethical implications could be sorted out. Stanford's Paul Berg won a Nobel Prize for his 1972 invention of the recombinant process, by which segments of DNA can be joined to other segments of DNA. The possibilities were staggering: for instance, normal genes could be "inserted into the cells of patients whose own genes lack the coding needed to stimulate production of disease-fighting hormones or enzymes."[6] Crops might be engineered so as to become resistant to insects or disease. The resultant Green revolution could feed the world.

In 1975, 140 of the world's top molecular biologists affirmed the potential benefits of recombinant DNA and wrote the guidelines under which such work should be conducted. The worries dissipated, and the worriers vanished. After all, as science writer Ronald Bailey notes, it was discovered that "organisms naturally exchange DNA among themselves."[7] James Watson, the biologist who with his partner Francis Crick first identified DNA in 1953, was one prominent advocate of the two-year moratorium. After which he pronounced himself worry-free: "Scientifically, I was a nut," he said in 1978. "There's no evidence at all that recombinant DNA poses the slightest danger."[8]

The promise of biotech remains bright but unmet. Of historic recombinant DNA experiments conducted in the early 1990s Dr. W. French Anderson of the National Heart, Lung and Blood Institute remarked, "This is the first step toward developing treatments that do not now exist for incurable diseases. There is a whole range of diseases that can be affected, the most immediately obvious being genetic diseases and cancer. Right behind them are AIDS and cardiovascular disease."[9]

More prosaic biotech advances, such as BGH, have stumbled. Not in the lab, mind you, but at the cash register. It comes as not the slightest surprise that Jeremy Rifkin was credited by *Forbes* with having "browbeaten"[10] five supermarket chains as well as Kraft, Dean Foods, and Dannon into banning milk from BGH-treated cows.

The biotech industry is in a virtual panic over the effect that Rifkin and Co. have had in poisoning the public mind. "I'm scared to death that one day Rifkin will show up on the *Today Show* holding a transgenic tomato that he says has toxins in it," says David Glass of BioTechnica Agriculture, Inc. "Yes, the tomato contains toxins, but they're not toxic to humans."[11]

But toxic is a potent word. As is gene. And clone. And, given its association with the Holocaust, eugenics.

Now, the dictionary definition holds that eugenics is the study or advocacy of "human improvement" by "selective breeding." Cross Aryan sperm with Aryan egg and produce a runner who gets left in the dust by Jesse Owens. A repugnant doctrine, but it has nothing to do with biotechnology.

Nevertheless, Jeremy Rifkin has gotten considerable mileage out of his belief that "Once we decide to begin the process of human genetic engineering, there is really no logical place to stop. If diabetes, sickle cell anemia, and cancer are to be cured by altering the genetic make-up of an individual, why not proceed to other 'disorders': myopia, color blindness, left handedness?"[12]

In other words, do nothing about diabetes, sickle cell anemia, and cancer: simply let the sufferers die, just because in the wild fantasies of the terminally fearful, this marvelous tool could be used for malignant purposes.

Rifkin claims that biotech "undermines the idea of the sacredness of life"[13]—though just how developing anti-corn-borer bacteria desacralizes life is quite beyond us. This is tied into his reverence for "species integrity," which, though very noble-sounding, is patently absurd. For as one scientist has noted, the eradication of smallpox "might have been a violation of species' integrity, but it was hardly mourned by any except possibly the smallpox virus itself."[14] Not everything that occurs in nature is benign; who will argue that "killing" the cancer cell is a hubristic instance of "playing God"? Try telling that to a cancer patient. The Executive Director of the Industrial Biotechnology Association has scorned Rifkin's stance as "an elitist attitude of someone who is not sick, who is not hungry, who is not suffering."[15]

Rifkin's Phony Populism

For one of Rifkin's most publicized protests, he showed up at a 1989 meeting of the National Institutes of Health's Recombinant DNA Advisory Committee accompanied by people in wheelchairs, the blind, and those with other disabilities. "You don't have people in this room who have a significant background in...disabilities,"[16] he charged in one *non sequitur*—after all, the meeting was devoted to consideration of a proposal (which was approved) to permit researchers to inject gene-altered cells into terminally ill cancer patients in an experimental treatment. "You cannot play God when it comes to deciding what genes should be engineered in and out of individual patients,"[17] thundered Rifkin, who, not having terminal cancer, attempted (unsuccessfully) to block the experiment with a lawsuit. (The lawsuit was settled when NIH agreed to pick up Rifkin's expenses. Being a gadfly can be fun when you don't have to pay the bills.) Now, isn't it Rifkin "playing God" by preventing or impeding human efforts to improve medical science?

Rifkin's pose as a populist is precious. This is the man who in 1992 announced, with the usual fanfare, a program called "Ticket America," under which an army of annoying nags were going to slap notices resembling traffic tickets onto the windshields of one million gas-guzzling cars, vans, and trucks. The tickets were intended to shame the drivers into trading in their gas hogs for compacts and "environmentally responsible" vehicles. Nowhere near one million were ever distributed; the project fizzled, for there are always many more chiefs than Indians in the nanny business.

A spokesman for the District of Columbia warned Rifkin and associates that each year about twenty District ticket-givers are assaulted by irate ticket-getters. But Jeremy Rifkin, whom no one has ever mistaken for Mike Tyson, was bursting with bravado. "We will not shy away from direct confrontation in the streets. I think a lot of people are going to be upset when their car is ticketed. I have no doubt about it."[18]

The late great populist voice of Chicago, Mike Royko, was having none of it. Admitting that his "grungy van probably qualifies as a gas guzzler," Royko issued this invitation to Rifkin:

> I will arrange to leave my car in a predetermined location, allowing Mr. Rifkin to issue a ticket accusing me of being politically incorrect and of having cruel and blatant disregard for the planet and unborn generations of little Rifkins.
>
> When he has written the ticket and put it under my wiper, I will leap out from behind the car, swat him with a tire iron, kick his ribs and jump up and down on his chest. Then I will slip a ticket into his pocket, accusing him of being a pain in the neck of society.[19]

As well as a neck-breaker. Researchers have determined that the Corporate Average Fuel Economy (CAFE) standards—the government-mandated fuel economy standard that each car maker must meet—are a threat to life and limb. Each increase in the required minimum fuel efficiency contributes to a higher death rate from accidents. To meet the requirements, automakers are forced to sell more small, which are less safe in a crash, than large cars.

But then extending the average person's life has never been a Rifkin priority.

The populist pose is also a sham because public opinion polls indicate that despite the misgivings fed by Rifkinite agitprop, most Americans welcome biotech—properly applied—as a blessing. A 1987 Louis Harris poll found that gene therapy to "cure a usually fatal genetic disease" was favored by 83 percent of respondents, and 84 percent supported treatments that would "stop children from inheriting a usually fatal disease."[20] Do not speak guff about "species integrity" to the parent of a child with sickle cell anemia.

Still, Jeremy Rifkin fights on. "He knows better than anybody how to use the political and legal systems for obstructionist purposes,"[21] says author Peter Huber. Through lawsuits and congressional testimony and freelance scaremongering, he has hamstrung an industry and planted within our minds the silliest and most disabling of questions: "What if?" And this despite the fact that "no one has gotten even so much as a sniffle"[22] from any biotech experiments gone wrong, as biotech industry executive Winston Brill says.

Rifkin does not seek to eliminate the risk, however minuscule that may be, of biotech; he aims to eliminate biotech itself. He cautioned Ronald Bailey in 1985 not to confuse him with the industry watchdogs or reformers who sought stricter regulation. "My position is not regulating it. It's not *wanting* it."[23]

And if Jeremy doesn't want it, the rest of us can't have it either. Who knows how many needless and painful deaths might have been prevented had biotech research proceeded at a reasonable pace over the past twenty years? What will posterity think of us? Ethicist Arthur Caplan told Bailey, "Three generations hence, people will think that worrying about biotechnology will be akin to our ancestors' worries about flying an airplane."[24]

But for now, Jeremy Rifkin is here, and he has a stage. "Crackpot or no crackpot, he has the public's ear, and he has to be reckoned with,"[25] as an EPA spokesman says. Meanwhile, biotech has been joined in Mr. Rifkin's rogue's gallery by that most inoffensive and placid of ruminants: the cow.

Beyond Common Sense

Rifkin has written a book cum gospel, *Beyond Beef*, which is a hodge-podge of outrageous claims against our bovine friends. Beef, it seems, is responsible for every ill in America and the world this side of the heartbreak of psoriasis. The elimination of beef would usher in a new world order of peace, harmony, and understanding, with liberty and justice for all—except, of course, for Ronald McDonald, whose harlequin head would finally meet the guillotine.

Shall we count the ways in which beef has ruined the earth and all living creatures, great and small?

Cattle are "wreaking havoc on the earth's ecosystems"[26]—six continents are being destroyed, by Rifkin's reckoning. The havoc is wreaked in every possible way: the rain forest is being leveled for mere pastureland; cattle herding is turning large chunks of sub-Saharan Africa, Australia, and the Western United States into virtual deserts; runoff from cattle feedlots is contaminating our groundwater. Cows' passing gas is even contributing to global warming.

And if all that environmental destruction is not enough, 70 percent of the world's grain is eaten by those ravenous, piggish cattle, while "as many as a billion people suffer from chronic hunger and malnutrition."[27] Millions of ignorant beef-eaters in the United States, Europe, and Japan are keeling over due to cancer, heart disease, and diabetes—all traceable to that scourge of mankind, that veritable masque of the red death: *beef.*

"Cattle production and beef consumption," warns Mr. Rifkin, "now rank among the gravest threats to the future well-being of the earth and its human population."[28]

Beyond Beef is a classic in the literature of unintentionally hilarious hysteria. To Rifkin, when the subject is the cow, no claim is too inflated, no crime too heinous. "Much of the religious and secular life of Western civilization has been erected on the broad shoulders of these powerful ungulates," he writes, awestruck. "The cow has been a useful projection and metaphor for defining our sense of self in the world as well as a utility for fashioning the world around us."[29] To which the skeptical reader can only respond: Bull.

"Ancient beef-eating myths and dietary practices have been used throughout history to maintain male dominance and establish gender and class hierarchies.... [B]eef eating has been used as a tool to forge national identity, advance colonial policies, and even promote racial theory."[30] At which point one slaps the forehead (one's own, not, alas, Rifkin's), and skips to the index, looking for "Hitler, Adolph," sure that the Holocaust will be laid at the feet of the poor cow, but then one remembers that the Führer was a vegetarian who shunned meat-eating, rather like...oh, never mind.

The bull, in the mind of man, is masculinity, aggression, a snorting and territorial creature; the cow is placidity with hooves. They are yin and yang, day and night, Laurel and Hardy. And so Mr. Rifkin leads us on a potted tour not easily forgotten: we are instructed on the ways of the bull worshippers of the kingdom of Narmer-Menes and the Egyptian belief in the cow goddess Hathor. We are shown the "industrial sewage" that cattle are fed today, and taken from the paintings of cattle ancestors in the French Lascaux caves to the cattle cults of the Middle East to the "Christian cultists" who administered the cruelest blow to the erstwhile bovine gods—the depiction of the devil himself as possessing cloven hooves. Hindus bathe sick children in cow urine; the Spaniards who flooded the New World with cattle—assisted by dastardly Catholic priests—established "a hierarchical herding culture, steeped in violence and subjugation and maintained by ruthless exploitation of native peoples and lands."[31] The beef-loving Englishmen who colonized the eastern rim of the New World were just as bad. And those Englishmen who stayed behind were every bit as evil: they indirectly caused the Irish potato famine by forcing the emerald isle to serve as mere pasturage for those damnable cattle.

History, to Rifkin, can be described as a running battle between pacific, nature-loving grain eaters and warlike herdsman—the first real "protocapitalists"[32]—who believe in war, conquest, and medium-rare steaks. Cattle herding was the product of an ethic of "ruthless acquisition" and "the cow, once a god, was slowly transformed into a commodity."[33] The "beef-eating overlords"[34] have spent millennia abusing grain-consuming peasants, and of course these brutes have actually tricked the peasantry into thinking that the rabble, too, should gobble down Big Macs while being oppressed. The cereal cultures of North Africa and the Middle East were the apex of culinary civilization: it's been all downhill since then, and the bottom, the pits, the valley of degeneracy, is populated by those who like fatty beef.

"Fatty beef" is to Jeremy Rifkin what Satan is to a fundamentalist preacher. Its mark is everywhere. When the working and middle classes in England began buying the fatty beef that had theretofore been all the rage among the aristocracy, the triumph belonged not to the butchers but to the cause of imperialism: "By consuming the fatty flesh of the bovine, these other classes signaled their willingness to take part in the colonial regime."[35]

Stateside, the depopulation of both buffalo and Indians from the western plains is the fault of...cattle. The buffalo were systematically slaughtered so that stupid cows could take their grassland; the Indians who depended on the buffalo were collateral damage, in the phrase of today's military. Meanwhile, a "powerful Euro-American cattle complex"[36] filled the West with vast cattle herds. And the Limey cattle barons, whose countrymen preferred the notorious fatty beef, coaxed Western cattlemen into fattening their four-legged chattel with surplus corn. And then there were the inventions: every advance in refrigeration is mourned by Rifkin as a loss of innocence, a loss of one-ness with nature—and never as a loss of rotted food.

(To be fair—and we won't mention the old line about the stopped clock—let us praise Rifkin on one point. He is absolutely right to condemn the century-old subsidized grazing privileges that ranchers have enjoyed on public lands in the American West.)

The reader who makes bold to remark that, just maybe, the widespread taste for beef is natural, and the reason cattle are so plentiful is that they are splendidly useful beasts, is soon set straight. "Americans are trained, from an early age, to gorge on beef,"[37] asserts Rifkin, who claims that "the average American consumes the meat of seven 1,100-pound steers in his or her lifetime."[38]

Asians have lagged behind Americans and Europeans in beef consumption, but a taste for this meat seems to go hand in hand with development. The Japanese have become ravenous beef-eaters, and the Koreans and Taiwanese are acquiring the taste. You might think that beef is therefore an edible symbol of success, but you miss the point, says Mr. Rifkin: for beef-eating imposes "new patterns of political dominance."[39]

Social dominance, too. Forget dogs; in Jeremy Rifkin's world, cows are a male chauvinist's best friend. He scorns middle-class America, in which the pathetic "'man' of the household lights up the charcoal and slaps the raw beef patties on the sizzling metal grill."[40] Roasting and consuming red meat, he argues, gives men the false impression that they are somehow more virile, more alive. Men use meat as a way of maintaining dominance over women. (No wisecracks, please.) Men are meat, women are vegetables, claims Rifkin, who says that the very language we use—a brain-dead person is called a "vegetable," to "beef up" is to become stronger—reinforces the male-meat patriarchal order.

Yes, in addition to all its other sins, the "beef culture" promotes "gender discrimination." In perhaps the most jaw-dropping sentence in a book which one reads with mouth ever agape, Rifkin writes, "Authorities report that many men use 'the absence of meat as a pretext for violence against women.'"[41] (The "authority" quoted is a book bearing the subtitle, *The Case Against the Patriarchy*, no doubt an even-handed treatment of the matter.) And get that "many." Do you, dear reader, know a single man who beats women because he's not eating meat? Does Jeremy Rifkin? If Rifkin and his "authority" are correct, then they've solved the problem of violence against women: just give all the spouse abusers meal vouchers to McDonald's.

As for McDonald's…well, don't worry about ever seeing Jeremy Rifkin ahead of you in the drive-through lane. With every quarter-pounder you buy, "the consumer secures a lien on the American world-view, its operating principles, vision, and goals."[42] And that's not including the pickle.

The ubiquity of McDonald's—Rifkin says that more than half the U.S. population lives within a three-minute drive of the Golden Arches—is, to Rifkin, a devastating comment on our countrymen. The arches themselves "bore a striking resemblance to pictorial images of the gates of heaven."[43] (Bet you didn't know that.) But Ray Kroc's chain occupies the lowest rung of Hell. Speed, uniformity, and the other hallmarks of a McDonald's restaurant may please some and dismay others, but to Rifkin this is not a question of taste; it's a theological matter, and he wants to deal with heretics—those who eat foods of which he disapproves—much as dogmatists have always dealt with recusants. A fellow meat-is-murder monk, columnist Colman McCarthy, refers to the supermarket meat counter as "a commercial cemetery for rotting animal parts,"[44] and when the language is that pungent you know that we're not talking about "I may disagree with what you say but I'd defend to the death your right to say it" guys.

No, Rifkin has not called for burning Big Mac eaters at the stake, yet. But they are culpable of great crimes, and great crimes are punished. "Chances are that the…teenagers gobbling down cheeseburgers at a fast-food restaurant will likely be unaware that a wide swath of tropical rain forest had to be felled and burned to bring them their meal,"[45] the high priest writes.

Now, that is simply not the case, and perhaps here is as good a place as any to begin setting the record straight by defending that most staid and reliable and occasionally tasty of beasts, the cow.

Let's Talk Cows—Home of the Deranged

Big Macs do not come direct from the rain forest. We import precious little beef, and what we do bring in is either canned or precooked. The U.S. imports no—none, nada, zilch—fresh beef from Brazil. (Some rain forest, i. e., jungle, was once cleared for pasturage, thanks to the bone-headed Brazilian government. The state subsidy responsible has since been repealed.)

Cattle, contrary to the lamentations of our Jeremy, are efficient beasts that turn grass into meat. "It takes an average of 4.5 pounds of grain to produce a pound of beef, retail weight."[46] They graze on land that is "too arid to support wheat, corn, or other food crops," writes journalist Tom Jackson. "If we all quit eating beef tomorrow, the environmental improvements would be minimal."[47]

And as for those flatulent cattle, mirth-making fodder for comedians around the globe, "a cow's impact on global warming is almost exactly that of a 75-watt light bulb."[48] Our domestic beef cattle, in all their rip-roaring glory, account for just one-half of one percent of world methane production and but 0.1 percent of total greenhouse gases. Rice paddies are bigger sources of methane production—but don't tell that to the rice and beans brigade.

Facts and figures and pesky numbers are not Rifkin's strong point. (Numbers are just so *Western*, don't you know?) He has claimed that it takes 2,400 gallons of water to produce one pound of steak—which is about 2,200 gallons too high. (By contrast, the "average household uses 107,000 gallons of water every year,"[49] notes the *Washington Post*, mischievously.) Reliable estimates of the amount of water consumed by U.S. beef cattle place it at two-tenths of one percent of the national total of annual water usage, and even that amount would decline if federal irrigation subsidies were eliminated.

In the literature of doomsaying, *Beyond Beef* makes even the grimmest eschatologists look like Pollyanna. For "a new neo-Malthusian threat looms before us, more frightening and sinister than anything that has come before."[50] More frightening and sinister than the Black Death? Than the Jewish Holocaust? The Cambodian Holocaust? The Armenian Holocaust? The Soviet gulag? The transoceanic slave trade? Yes. Far more so. The "transition of world agriculture from food grain to feed grains"—the result of our cattle culture, and the need to feed those one billion kine throughout the world—"represents a new form of human evil, whose consequences may be far greater and longer-lasting than any past examples of violence inflicted by men against their fellow human beings."[51]

The only way to forestall this unimaginable evil, says Rifkin, is to convert acreage now dedicated to pasturage or feed grain to...legumes and leafy vegetables! Yes, it's those damned lentils all over again!

Rifkin claims that over 70 percent of the grain produced by American farmers "is fed to livestock, primarily cattle."[52] Globally, the situation is not much better; piggish cattle are eating all the grain. "If worldwide agricultural production were shifted from livestock feed to grains for direct human consumption," Rifkin states, "more than a billion people could be fed."[53]

"The makings of a worldwide food crisis are already in the offing,"[54] warns Rifkin. Whole subcontinents are falling prey to "hordes of hoofed locusts in search of grass and grain." These cattle aren't merely denying food to the hungry—they're even "threatening millions of years of biological evolution"![55]

We live in a hideous world which features "a billion people gorging and purging, mired in excess fat, while a billion more waste away."[56] The reason is that one-third of the world's grain is fed to livestock: if only we had less livestock, we would have more healthy grain-fed people and fewer starvelings. There is only one problem with this argument: it is complete, unadulterated, non-grain-fed cowpatties.

Again, we have left the world of facts and numbers to fly in the clouds of Rifkin-land, unmoored to what we lesser souls call reality. In fact, more than 90 percent of the U.S. land used for grazing is unsuitable for cultivated crops. Moreover, year in and year out we have an enormous grain surplus: the problem is not that greedy cattle hog all the grain, it is that the command economies and kleptocracies of the Third World, aided and abetted by international development agencies, have, by their heavy-handed interventions, misallocated resources, destroyed traditional agrarian societies, and caused untold human misery. 'Tis kings, and not cows, who have starved Africa.

The world's annual grain surplus is about 200 million tons; our own government pays farmers *not* to use land for grain production. Domestic cattle consume just 11 percent of U.S.-produced grain, which hardly comports with the Rifkin's picture of cows pushing starving children away from the trough.

Just when Rifkin's poor beleaguered reader of Rifkin's rant thinks that the poor cow is to be untied from the whipping post, Rifkin levels yet another charge: cattle pose "one of the most destructive environmental threats of the modern era."[57] No, they don't smoke or drive cars, but that's because they're too busy "trampling the soil, stripping the vegetation bare, laying waste to large tracts of the earth's biomass."[58] They deplete the water supply; their dung pollutes our rivers and streams; they run riot over the rain forests; they erode soil. Think of them as four-legged businessmen.

Of course the government-subsidized clearing of small parts of the rain forest is a mistake; the criminals, in this case, are the Brazilian government and the international development agencies that support it. The fault lies not in the cow, dear Rifkin, but in the state. The same is true of federally subsidized irrigation in the West; ranchers *are* propped up by the feds, to an extent, and if Rifkin focused his energies on ending such subsidies he would—indirectly—further his cause. But then saving the taxpayers a few billion is not what is on Jeremy Rifkin's mind: it is changing the collective diet; removing beef from America's plates and substituting legumes.

Rifkin's patchwork of absurdities boggles the mind. Soil erosion cannot be laid at the cloven hooves of cattle; if anything, devoting land to forage rather than cultivated crops helps *conserve* soil. The amount of fossil fuel necessary to produce seventy pounds of beef, which is the average per capita consumption in the United States, is between 10.9 and 15.4 gallons—which is what you'll use next time you fill 'er up at the service station. Almost all cattle manure ends up as natural fertilizer on the land. Cattle are, in fact, among the most environmentally correct of beasts: "more than 99 percent of the energy used"[59] to produce them comes from none other than the sun.

"Dismantling the global cattle complex and eliminating beef from the diet of the human race is an essential task of the coming decades if we are to have any hope of restoring our planet to health and feeding a growing human population,"[60] asserts Rifkin. Yet Professor L.M. Schake of the University of Connecticut notes that the cattle complex, and corn complex, and poultry complex, and wheat complex, and all those other agricultural complexes that have given Jeremy Rifkin his complex, are to thank for the very size of the human population. "Maximum sustainable population of humans would be approximately 20 to 30 million people if hunting/gathering hadn't been replaced with organized agriculture,"[61] says Dr. Schake.

But then Jeremy Rifkin always wants it both ways. He condemns nineteenth-century Englishmen for hogging all the tasty beef while "women and children 'eat the potatoes and look at the meat.'"[62] Yet by his accounting beef is the great killer of our age; so weren't these English men doing the women and children a favor?

Like the scolding scarecrows of CSPI, Jeremy Rifkin sings loudly in the thin-is-beautiful choir. Beef-eating nations produce "fat, often obese"[63] people, gluttonous participants at the saturnalia of excess that is our civilization. Anorexia, bulimia, the mounds of fat hanging over your next-door neighbor's belt: Blame it all on beef! "Unable to reconcile their historical lust for animal fat with their new streamlined self-image, [Americans] remain betwixt and between an orgy of consumption and purging unique in human experience."[64]

The "Meat Is Murder" Theory

Rifkin buys into every health threat ever attached to beef: colon cancer, heart disease, breast cancer…. "Americans and Europeans are literally eating themselves to death, gorging on marbled beef and other grain-fed animal products"[65] instead of eating cereal like the peaceful cultures of the non-Western world.

In fact, researchers generally agree that there is *no* association between meat intake and colon cancer (or any other type of cancer). Marvin Harris, writing for the New York Academy of Sciences, states, "The basic reason why heart disease and cancer have become the number one and number two causes of death in the United States and other affluent countries is that people are living longer…. What has allowed us to live long enough to run these risks? Meat, among other things. The increased consumption of animal foods and decreased consumption of grains are strongly associated with increased longevity."[66] Take *that*, gentle cereal-eaters of the Third World!

Rifkin's Beyond Beef Coalition has declared, in full-page newspaper ads, that "aside from smoking, there is no greater personal health risk than eating meat."[67] Although this is a useful hint that should tip us off to the Rifkin agenda of the early twenty-first century—warning labels on burger wrappers?—Tufts University professor of nutrition Jeanne Goldberg scoffed, "to talk about smoking and beef in the same sentence is nonsense."[68]

Indeed, meat most certainly is nutritious. Animal foods supplies us bipeds with 68 percent of the protein, 83 percent of the calcium, 60 percent of the phosphorous, 42 percent of the iron, and almost all of the vitamin B-12 we need. No one this side of the most demented vegetotalitarian argues than lean beef is harmful; indeed, lean cuts of beef have been recommended for those "seeking to lower their blood cholesterol levels."[69] Beef is rich in protein and easily absorbable iron. Even the usual suspects—the American Cancer Society, the American Dietetic Association, the American Heart Association—endorse lean meat for the dinner table.

Studies have repeatedly indicated that children bred on a vegetarian diet are smaller than those who consume the seared flesh of murdered animals. Women, especially, with their higher iron requirements, ought to tear into a steak now and then. As *Prevention Magazine* declared, "Red meat contains substantial amounts of copper, manganese and zinc. These three minerals work together with calcium to prevent the brittle-bone condition known as osteoporosis. Beef, in particular, is a veritable banquet for the bones; it's high in copper and manganese...and a good source of zinc."[70]

(But wait—put that fork down! For there, in the distance, is the ominous specter of "cow AIDS," or bovine immunodeficiency virus. You probably haven't heard of this. But Rifkin raises the possibility that those kine stricken with this weakening of the immune system may somehow pass the virus on to humans, causing those who consume milk or beef from the infected cattle to become HIV- positive. A horrid thought—and one that seems to occupy only the feverish mind of Jeremy Rifkin.)

Like ants at the picnic, the Center for Science in the Public Interest has showed up at this squabble, verbally barbecuing the beef industry. The inimitable *Nutrition Action Healthletter* warns:

> *Don't eat ground beef and other fatty meats.* Red meat is the largest source of fat and saturated fat in the average American's diet. The saturated fat alone makes it Heart Disease Enemy No. 1. Among the fattiest are ribs, bacon, and sausage. But the worst is ground beef...because we eat more of it than any other red meat."[71]

If Rifkin and CSPI were really interested in consumer safety they would support irradiation of beef, but, well, that would break the mold, and neo-puritans are nothing if not orthodox. Instead of praising irradiation, Rifkin keeps the lawyers swimming in billable hours, filing suits like the one that resulted in a 1993 U.S. Department of Agriculture directive that raw meat labels must instruct readers to "cook thoroughly." Duh, you say, but "cook thoroughly" was "open to too much interpretation,"[72] mewled Rifkin, who demanded labels that instruct cooks to burn every last particle of pinkness from the rotting animal carcass which they are about to consume as a symbolic act of Western male hegemony. He urged the federal government require restaurants to char beef to at least 160 degrees—no more medium-rare steak, and, in the fondest dreams of *Beyond Beef*, a resultant decline in beef consumption.

Rifkin's Real Agenda

And this, of course, is the real goal of the Beyond Beef movement. What Rifkin really wants is to put McDonald's out of business. His Beyond Beef campaign, which sought to cut world beef consumption in half, leafletted (by its own highly suspect estimate) one million customers of the Golden Arches, disturbing their digestion with the suggestion that hamburgers were a raw deal for your health, the cow, and the earth. Beyond Beef demanded that McDonald's start selling a vegetarian burger, which would be only slightly more profitable than launching a new line of *E. coli* cheeseburgers. Consumers simply do not want veggie burgers. The McLean, which the company promoted heavily in the early 1990s as the low-fat alternative to a Big Mac, flopped, in part because people found out that water and a seafood extract known as carrageenan served as mortar to hold the patty together. Mmm-mmm good: Who can turn down a seafood extract and water patty with a side order of fries?

Beyond Beef upped its effrontery ante by demanding that McDonald's devote one-quarter of its advertising budget to the hypothetical veggie burger. In the meantime, it demanded that television stations air its own anti-beef ads *for free*: Does "chutzpa" even begin to capture the essence of Rifkin?

"This campaign is not about beef, it's about Rifkin's desire to police American stomachs," thundered Rick Perry, Texas commissioner of agriculture. "It'll take more than stomach police to convince the public that the hamburger is responsible for everything from sexual discrimination to racism."[73]

Beef cattle is a $40 billion industry in these United States. Unlike, say, the dairy farmers of Vermont for whom Jeremy Rifkin bleeds, cattlemen are not propped up by a price support system. They have succeeded because people like to eat beef, and no matter how loudly the nannies hector, the scraping of plates and ringing of cash registers is all the vindication that our much-maligned cattle need.

In the end, perhaps the corrosive acid of ridicule is the best weapon with which to defend the all-American hamburger patty. Author

Laurence Leamer, mind boggled by Rifkin's *Beyond Beef*, took pen in hand and wrote the *Washington Post*:

> I say not only beyond beef. I say beyond fish, beyond fruit and beyond vegetables.
>
> Anyone who has seen, as I have, the almost human look of a flounder brutally pulled out of the sea, gasping on the floor of a boat, would never eat a fish fillet again. And pity the humble endive, who has wished no one harm. Perhaps the worst, however, is the fate of the potato, that gentle, low-lying tuber. Farmers pull its eyes out and plant them in the ground. It is pulled out of its earthy home at a time when it is thinking only of reproduction, thrown into a sack, and carted hundreds, sometimes thousands of miles from home. Then it is skinned alive, cut into pieces and fried, dropped into vats of boiling water, or baked in ovens.
>
> Let us join, then, with [Colman] McCarthy and Rifkin and not only bypass the meat counter, but the displays of dead and dying fruits and vegetables. Let us pledge to end the wasteful, inhumane, ugly business of eating and get on with life.[74]

Amen. And make ours rare.

8

Whose Life Is It, Anyhow?

The control of the material means of pro-
duction is a social function, subject to the
confirmation or revocation by the sovereign
consumer. This is what the modern concept of
freedom means. Every adult is free to fashion
his life according to his own plans.
—Ludwig von Mises
The Anti-Capitalistic Mentality

Liberty not only means that the individual has
both the opportunity and the burden of choice;
it also means that he must bear the conse-
quences of his actions and will receive praise
or blame for them. Liberty and responsibility
are inseparable.
—F.A. Hayek
The Constitution of Liberty

Should we throw people in jail for being fat? Seriously, should we? The question seems preposterous. Throw fat people in jail? Impossible. Why, the next thing you know we'd be filling the hoosegow with people who make their own whiskey or smoke hemp. On second thought....

The neo-puritans are quick to say that they've learned their lesson from Prohibition, but have they? The language of individual choice and personal liberty is nowhere evident in the publications of MADD or CSPI. Those who dislike cigarette smoking have become emboldened enough to speak openly of the eventual prohibition of the demon weed. You start with children, of course, and then ban such things as advertisements, which are aimed at adults but might be seen by children, and you then forbid adults to traffic in or use the substance because it might have second-hand or tertiary effects upon children, and before you know it, the evil cigarette/liquor/cheese doodle is being extirpated from America by the agents of the Bureau of Alcohol, Tobacco, and Firearms (and Fritos?).

As Richard Klein writes:

> After alcohol and tobacco, now fat has been proscribed. America, under the spur of its persistent Puritanism, cruelly medicalizes the matter of public health and social morality, of disease and compulsion. The health industry has already deemed food to be medicine, and fat is poison. That industry, with its ally, the government, is about to turn fat into a drug, which will give it the absolute control it desires, not only over occasional pleasures, like tobacco or liquor, but over food itself, which has the peculiarly profitable quality, distinct from that of any other drug, of being indispensable to life. The drumbeat of moralizing around food is rising to feverish intensity.[1]

The clampdown may be closer than you think. Dr. Kelly Brownell, director of the Yale Center for Eating and Weight Disorders, has been quoted as saying, "I don't want to rule out any approaches"[2] in the war on fat. Surely he spoke carelessly, right? Maybe. Or maybe not. For Dr. Brownell may well be a white-smocked harbinger of the next great government undertaking. Yes, from the folks who brought you the War on Poverty, the War in Vietnam, and the War on Drugs comes...The War on Fat!

In the pages of the *New York Times*, Brownell has called for "taxing low-nutrition foods." He has even worked out his own fatty-foods tax system, under which foods "would be judged on their nutritive value per calorie or gram of fat; the least healthy would be given the highest tax rate. Consumption of high-fat food would drop, and the revenue could be used for middle and upper-middle class amenities such as "bike paths and running tracks."[3] (The next step, presumably, will be to require all of us flabby slobs to hit the track at least three times a week under penalty of imprisonment or, in the case of really hard cases, the force-feeding of lentils.)

As night follows day, Dr. Brownell buttresses his bizarre social-engineering scheme with appeals to "the children." The young folk, he writes—though clearly he would include kids from one to ninety-two in their number—"can't make mature decisions in the face of clever commercials and should not be inundated with temptations to eat some of the most processed, calorie-rich, fat-laden foods on the planet."[4] So as we await deliverance day, when fat shall be taxed out of existence, we can in the meantime ban television and radio ads for foods that Dr. Brownell finds unhealthy. (Don't bother looking for references to the

First Amendment or such trifles as freedom of speech in Brownell's manifestos. And need we add that Dr. Brownell is on the Scientific Advisory Board of the unavoidable CSPI?)

Richard Klein, for one, is unconvinced:

> To the already bloated bureaucracy, Dr. Brownell would add a fat czar. With the best intentions in the world, the Yale nutritionist would make the fat pay sin taxes for their pleasures, raising monies to be used to finance the activities of the thin. The thin, who already are likely to be the rich, would get another tax break; the poor, likely to be fat, would be of the object of the government's tough love.... This latest proposal seems rather like the logical outcome of the whole current wave of anti-fat propaganda, raised to an even more hysterical pitch and leading to even scarier demands for action. In the minds of these well-meaning scientists, fat is such a danger to the body politic that it warrants further government intrusions into people's lives, and additional confiscation of their wealth. Nowhere in all this talk of taxing fat food do we hear a single good word for the blessing of chocolate, the balm of chicken soup, or the comfort of a nicely schmeared bagel."[5]

We Smell a Rat

Brownell betrays his something less than elevated view of his fellow human beings when he notes: "Laboratory rats given convenience store delights—cheese curls, chocolate bars, marshmallows, cookies—will ignore available nutritious food, even as their body weight doubles and triples. Yet we do not fault these animals for a lack of discipline, nor need we change their biology. Remove bad foods, and the rats stay thin."[6]

Remove bad foods (as defined by the Brownells and Jacobsons) from our dinner tables, and we human rats will stay thin. What can one say about a man so obsessed (dare we say consumed?) by hatred of a few extra pounds that he has come to regard the rest of us as nothing more than biped rats whose masters can slip bowls of what they think is good for us into our cages and we'll eat it without a squeak of protest? Not surprisingly, Brownell decries the emphasis on "personal responsibility" for obesity. He also seems rather wistful about the failure of Prohibition to take root in America. "There is not sufficient political will in the United States to ban the sale of tobacco nor to ban the sale of alcohol," he laments, "yet we realize they carry tremendous social burdens, so we tax them to increase the price and decrease the use. Why can't the same thing happen with food?"[7]

Well, Dr. Brownell, do not despair. Your dream may yet come true. As the old American liberties give way to the custodial state, which takes care of us in return for the forfeiture of our personal rights and our freedom, the taxing of fat people and perhaps, eventually, their incarceration, where they can subsist on prison diets of brown rice until they're just the right size and have been re-educated to crave tofu (in modest amounts, natch!) may be just around the corner.

We have had fun with the prohibitionists and nannies; their more fevered utterances read like clever, if over-the-top, parodies; but at base, what these people demand is not funny at all. They want power, they want total control, and if a few human rats have to be squashed in the process—well, that's life. One must break a few eggs to make an omelet. And a gray and colorless life it will be, with no savor, no flavor, just compulsion and grim joyless feeding and the clang of the jailhouse doors for those who resist.

In the early 1980s, Allan Luks, neo-prohibitionist director of the New York City affiliate of the National Council on Alcoholism, wrote a book titled *Will America Sober Up?* A significant title: not will Americans sober up, but will America sober up: 250 million of us are submerged into one huge drunken continental blob. Mr. Luks said, "Not too long ago, we thought Americans were heavy drinkers, and that many of them just wanted to kill themselves with it. But now we see that they want change, and that they are looking to the government for direction."[8]

You sure said a mouthful, Mr. Luks. "Americans," you will notice, are not "us" but "them." Which nation Mr. Luks claims citizenship in we do not know; technically, no doubt, it is the United States, but in practice he wishes to separate himself from the besotted, begrimed hordes, who live only to drink, and drink only to live. But perhaps they're not lost souls after all, for they "want change." Not that they're willing to change themselves, mind you. That, we know, would be quite impossible, for the individual will is not capable of denying the body a glass of beer or wine. No, "they are looking to the government for direction." Like children, they must be led. Not by father or mother, mind you, but by the mother of all mothers: the Nanny State.

To call these people "do-gooders" is to give them far too much credit. They are not do-gooders, they are bullies, and cowardly bullies at that, eager to drag in the coercive arm of the state to fight their battles for them. They should be mocked, hooted at, and battled every step of the way.

When that epitome of the individualist American, Henry David Thoreau, came back from the woods near Walden Pond, he pronounced "reformers...the greatest bores of all." For they just won't let you be.

"I did not fear the hen-harriers," wrote Henry, "for I kept no chickens; but I feared the men-harriers rather."[9]

The men-harriers today operate with powers that poor Thoreau never dreamed of. We may still enjoy a dish of ice cream, a bottle of beer, or a plate of fettucini Alfredo in our little Waldens, but the neo-puritans are at the door. They want in, and they want our pleasures out. What are we going to do about it?

On a More Sober Note

We have been highly critical of the food and drink police, even ridiculing them as self-appointed nannies, busybodies, and petty tyrants. We have done this because, frankly, they deserve it. There is much more at stake here than how much tax one will pay on one's twinkies, how many beers one may safely consume at Pizza Hut after a softball game, or the character of Budweiser ads. What is at issue is how much personal responsibility Americans should assume for their own behavior and, consequently, how much personal freedom they will enjoy.

Is government our servant—as the classical theory of democracy informs us—or has it become our master, having given itself the power to control everything we put into our bodies, if not our minds? Is pervasive regulatory regimentation of everyone's life the only feasible way of dealing with health risks? Is the essence of American business really profiting by selling dangerous or deadly products to an unsuspecting public? This is the theory of capitalism that seems to inform virtually all of the individuals and groups we have labeled the food and drink police.

Freedom and Responsibility

The epigram at the beginning of this final chapter taken from the late F.A. Hayek is one of the most powerful statements that the great man ever made. A free society cannot function, Hayek explained, unless its members accept the fact that they are responsible for their own actions. Yes, accidents over which we have no control happen, but the point is that a society where individual responsibility is the norm tends to direct the citizen's attention "to those circumstances that he can control as if they were the only ones that mattered...."[10] The regulatory assaults on individual choice that we have catalogued in this book are nothing less than assaults on our fundamental freedoms. They can only succeed if Americans are willing to throw in the towel with regard to personal responsibility and become, like idiot children, effective wards of the state when it comes to deciding what to eat, drink, read, spend their money on, and even think.

The motivations of the food and drink police are clear: the more responsibility *they* have for determining our consumption choices, the more power and wealth they will accumulate. Government regulators will enjoy greater power and larger budgets, and the various "nonprofit" organizations, such as MADD and CSPI, will likely share in the bounty of tax revenues procured through ever-increasing excise taxes on politically incorrect consumer goods. The pipe dream of the food and drink police has to be, ultimately, to do to the beer, wine, liquor, and fast-food industries what the anti-smoking lobby did to the tobacco industry—essentially extorting hundreds of billions of dollars from it. It is not out of the question, by any means, to expect to hear arguments being made that since so many people have become ill or have died from overeating and overdrinking—or from "bad" diets—that these *industries* should be made to pay "society" billions of dollars in health care reparations.

Such arguments can only be accepted if one abandons the notion of individual responsibility and absolves those who engage in overeating, overdrinking, and other forms of unhealthy behavior from all responsibility. It is disconcerting that Hayek noted *almost forty years ago* that the belief in individual responsibility "has markedly declined, together with the esteem for freedom" and "has become an unpopular concept, a word that experienced speakers or writers avoid because of the obvious...animosity with which it is received by a generation that dislikes all moralizing."[11] So-called moral relativism is not a "new" phenomenon; Hayek wrote those words in the late 1950s.

We take it as a self-evident truth that mentally healthy adults have free will and a consciousness that enables them to foresee the likely consequences of their actions. As such, they can and should be held responsible for their own behavior, good or bad.

In contrast, the philosophy of the food and drink police seems to be the nineteenth-century notion that "social forces," not free will, guide individual behavior. This latter philosophy is at the heart of virtually all of the social policy disasters of the twentieth century, from fascism, socialism, and communism, to the soft-on-crime crusade that began in the 1960s and the failed "war" on poverty. The poor are said to be poor because of forces beyond their control. Criminals are said to be all but blameless for the crimes they commit, for the "root causes" of crime, we have all been told, are such things as poverty and discrimination, not criminal behavior. Such convoluted thinking deserves howls of derision and ridicule in light of the social policy debacles it has encouraged.

Respecting the dignity of other people requires that we tolerate the choices of others, as long as those choices do not harm us or interfere with our own freedoms. We should be free to criticize the choices of others, but that is altogether different from having the government ban or restrict other peoples' choices of which we happen to disapprove. For we all have our vices; once it becomes "legitimate" for government to ban, restrict, regulate, or control one vice, then in principle there is no stopping it; all personal freedom is at risk. Only a totalitarian government can effectively control all personal choices that someone perceives as "risky" or undesirable.

Moreover, granting more or less monopoly powers to government agencies like the FDA or the BATF is risky in itself. For monopolistic government agencies are notorious for their inefficiency, incompetence, and corruption, all of which can make life *more* risky.

The FDA, for example, has greatly expanded the number of years required to place new drugs on the market because of its bureaucratic inertia. Consequently, many lives have been lost and much suffering has occurred as American citizens have been deprived for years of life-saving drugs that had long been available elsewhere in the world. The FDA finally approved the use of irradiation on meat products in 1997, for example, but only after hundreds of Americans died of *E. coli* poisoning that could have been prevented by a more widespread use of irradiation. The risks of bureaucratic ineptitude (if not outright tyranny) can be far greater than the risks of eating beef—a practice that has apparently terrified Jeremy Rifkin—or enjoying Italian, Mexican, and Chinese food, a pastime that is strongly discouraged by the scarecrow-like figures at CSPI.

For many decades now, Americans have been seduced by government agencies into giving up more and more of their freedoms *and responsibilities* in return for *promises* of greater safety and security, courtesy of the nanny state. Charles Murray discusses in great detail in his book, *In Pursuit: Of Happiness and Good Government*, how government action has displaced private initiative time and time again, to the detriment of society.[12] When government essentially took over the practice of providing assistance to the poor, more and more Americans decided it was not their role to become concerned about the families in their communities who did not have enough to eat or sufficient housing; the government would supposedly take care of it all.

When government monopolized the old-age insurance industry, people responded by saving less for their own retirement and providing less assistance to their own parents and grandparents in their old age; the government would ostensibly take care of them.

When government monopolized public education, many parents became much less involved in their childrens' education, leaving it all up to governmental "experts." When government came to dominate product safety regulation, people came to believe that as long as a product has been government inspected, it must be safe.

Now that the welfare state is a universally acknowledged failure, the public schools in many cities are a disgrace, regulation routinely imposes billions of dollars of costs on society without any detectable benefits, and the Social Security and Medicare systems are on the brink of bankruptcy, Americans are left without all the "little platoons," as Edmund Burke once described them, of voluntary, community-based groups that were once so effective at resolving individual or neighborhood problems and difficulties. Life has become much riskier thanks to the "security" of big government. And it is even bigger government that the food and drink police want to impose on us.

The Search for Safety

The incessant clamor for higher excise taxes, advertising and product bans, and more government regulation in general on the part of the food and drink police is a consequence of a gross misunderstanding of the nature of economic relationships in capitalistic economies. The marketplace can best be thought of as "a dynamic process of discovery generated by the entrepreneurial-competitive scramble for pure profit."[13] Competition stimulates a process of *discovery,* whereby business firms realize profits by uncovering previously uncovered means of satisfying consumers. Competition creates a constant quest to discover new knowledge that is applicable to serving consumers better than one's competitors, including discovering ways of making products cleaner, safer, and better overall, for those are attributes for which consumers are willing to pay.

It is well known that government regulation of market relationships more often than not backfires because of the Law of Unintended Consequences. Rent control laws intended to help the poor only make the poor worse off by creating housing shortages; the minimum wage law is intended similarly to help the poor, but harms them instead by pricing them out of jobs; federal deposit insurance regulation was supposed to make banking less risky, but made it more risky instead by encouraging bankers to make more risky loans, with the understanding that bad loans would be subsidized by federal insurance. The list of counterproductive regulation is long, indeed.

A more important failure of regulation, however, is that it tends to stifle the entrepreneurial discovery process that is a normal part of the marketplace. Whenever government steps in and imposes product quality standards, for example, the incentive is for businesses to meet those standards, but not much more. By contrast, in an unregulated, competitive marketplace the struggle for profit results in ever-increasing standards. Regulation tends to freeze in place one governmentally defined standard of quality and to cut short the entrepreneurial discovery process. Improved safety and other desirable product characteristics must be *discovered*. The pretense of government regulation is that such knowledge is already known by a group of government experts (and perhaps by nonprofit sector activists at CSPI and elsewhere).

In a competitive marketplace there are enormous pressures to continually improve product quality and safety, especially in today's global economy. And in the marketplace there are handsome rewards—in the form of profits—for businesses which do so. At the same time there are penalties—in the form of lost profits or bankruptcy—for companies that fail to do so.

But there are no profit-and-loss incentives, as such, facing government regulators. In fact, as has been discussed in the context of FDA regulation, many regulators tend to be extremely conservative in order to preserve their jobs and budgets. For example, at the FDA the incentive is to be excessively cautious, because allowing a food or drug product onto the market that has dangerous side effects creates terrible publicity for the agency and may threaten its budgetary expansion. On the other hand, delaying the introduction of valuable drugs for years rarely creates a problem *for the agency*. It is the potential users of the drugs who have the problem. Because this process imposes such enormous financial costs on drug companies (and their customers), there is far less innovation, research, and development of new products than would occur in a free market. There is also far less competition, for the high cost of complying with government regulation often drives smaller competitors from the market and discourages others from entering the market in the first place.

We will never know what kind of "miracle drugs" might have been invented were it not for FDA regulation and its imposition of government-enforced criteria on drug manufacturers. In a free market, the only criteria that count are criteria that work—ones that result in new drugs that produce desirable medical results and can therefore earn profits for the drugs' manufacturers. The stifling of the market process is one of the major (though unmeasurable) costs of regulation.

Regulation alters the *pattern* of entrepreneurial discovery away from one that is purely driven by consumer sovereignty to one that is driven by the whims of government bureaucrats.[14] A good example is how the automobile industry has been induced to spend enormous resources engineering smaller cars in order to meet the government's CAFE standards, which mandate that each automaker's fleet must average a government-prescribed miles-per-gallon requirement (currently about 25 mpg). There has been no significant consumer demand for smaller cars; quite the opposite—the fastest-selling segment of the automobile market is minivans, light trucks, and sports utility vehicles, which account for almost half of all automobile sales in the United States. And since, as of this writing, the price of gasoline is the lowest it has been in several decades, the demand for *larger* cars is likely to grow. Nevertheless, in order to meet regulatory requirements enacted during the (government-created) energy crisis of the 1970s—which was essentially over by 1980—America's automotive engineers and their employers are compelled to spend untold thousands of man-hours and unimaginable sums of money "discovering" the means of manufacturing smaller and smaller cars, even though few Americans want to buy them.

Finally, it should also be pointed out that one further result of the pervasive regulation of virtually everything in American life is an increased degree of bribery and corruption of regulators and politicians. American corporations spend large sums of money and inordinate man-hours lobbying legislatures for favorable regulatory treatment for themselves and, at times, for unfavorable treatment for their competitors. This wasteful activity is another undesirable, unforeseen, and unintended consequence of the kind of regulatory agenda promoted by the food and drink police.

The Role of "Greed"

The philosophical basis of all the food and drink police do is the notion that, left to their own devices, business people will generally sell unsafe food and drugs, commit fraud, and offer shoddy products in general. Thus, we are supposedly in need of the "services" of our self-appointed national nannies and the government regulatory agencies they support (and are supported by).

The fatal flaw in this philosophy is its failure to recognize that it is precisely the "greed" of business people that is the surest guarantor of ever safer and healthier products. As Alan Greenspan once observed, "it is in the self-interest of every businessman to have a reputation for honest dealings and a quality product. Since the market value of a going business is measured by its money-making potential, reputation or 'good will' is as much an asset as its physical plant and equipment."[15] Reputation is a major competitive tool, and businesses that offer consumers unsafe products risk a quick demise. This is not to say that there will never be unsafe or unhealthy products on the market, but that the competitive marketplace provides all the "right" incentives as far as product safety is concerned.

Government regulation, on the other hand, undercuts the value of reputation by placing a disreputable (but government-licensed) company on the same basis as one that has earned the trust of consumers with decades of good performance. It also relieves consumers of the "trouble" of investing the time and effort it takes to investigate a company or product; the government's word or license is used as a substitute. The government's minimum standards have a way of becoming maximum standards and, as already mentioned, such standards invite bribery of public officials by companies who want to be designated as government-approved. As Greenspan explained by way of example: "A fly-by-night securities operator can quickly meet all the [Securities and Exchange Commission] requirements, gain the inference of respectability, and proceed to fleece the public. In an unregulated economy, the operator would have had to spend a number of years in reputable dealings before he could earn a position of trust sufficient to induce a number of investors to place funds with him."[16] Government regulation does not eliminate dishonest business people; it only makes them harder to detect. It relies on fear and coercion, rather than incentives, which is why it so often fails to achieve its stated objectives.

A Nation of Mentally Challenged Children?

One of the authors recently appeared on the Fox News television channel in New York City to discuss a topic somewhat related to the substance of this book—the activities of the tobacco prohibitionists. He commented on the air that the premise behind all such neo-prohibitionist movements seems to be that all American adults should be viewed as mentally immature children who need to be led around by their noses (figuratively speaking, of course) by an enlightened regulatory elite. This view of adults is simply not valid, your author argued, to which the host of the television show, a former network news anchor, responded in a raised voice: "But they are! They *are* like children!"

This outburst is not likely to have endeared the host to his audience, but it is a telling story of how so many well-educated Americans have fallen for the idea that, although they themselves are wise and well educated, the rest of us should indeed be treated by the state as ignorant and helpless children. Too many Americans have accepted this view, in our opinion, because they believe it relieves them of the responsibility of taking charge of their own lives and their own health. As more Americans come to believe this, we will travel farther and farther along the path of having a government that is the master, rather than the servant, of the people. Socialism may be dead, but in its place is a degree of regulatory regimentation that may eventually prove just as destructive to our prosperity and our freedom, thanks in part to the self-important zealots known as the food and drink police.

Notes

Chapter 1

1. Richard Klein, *Eat Fat* (New York: Pantheon, 1996), p. 108.
2. Stephen Glass, "Hazardous to Your Mental Health," *New Republic* (30 December 1996), p. 18.
3. Victor Gold, "Damn the Food Police!" *Washingtonian* (October 1994), p. 55. This article is an interview of Robert Shoffner, the food and wine critic of *Washingtonian* magazine.
4. "You Have a Golden Opportunity," (Wilmington, DE: MBNA America Bank, 1992), brochure promoting Center for Science in the Public Interest Gold MasterCard.
5. Glass, "Hazardous to Your Mental Health," pp. 19–20.
6. Gold, "Damn the Food Police!" p. 57.
7. Bonnie Liebman, "A Dozen Dos & Don'ts," *Nutrition Action Healthletter* (Washington, DC: Center for Science in the Public Interest, June 1996), p. 12.
8. ibid.
9. ibid.
10. Glass, "Hazardous to Your Mental Health," pp. 16–17.
11. Quoted in David Shaw, *The Pleasure Police* (New York: Doubleday, 1996), p. 52.
12. ibid., p. 54.
13. Liebman, "A Dozen Dos and Don'ts," p. 13.
14. Carole Sugarman, "Who Is Michael Jacobson and Why Won't He Let Us Eat Our Chinese Food and French Fries in Peace?" *Washington Post*, 27 October 1993, p. E4.
15. ibid.
16. Quoted in Glass, "Hazardous to Your Mental Health," p. 18.
17. Sugarman, "Who Is Michael Jacobson…," p. E4.
18. ibid.
19. Glass, "Hazardous to Your Mental Health," p. 18.
20. "Center for Science (or Politics?) in the Public Interest," *Organization Trends* (Washington, DC: Capital Research Center, September 1991), pp. 3–4.
21. Asra Q. Nomani and Gabriella Stern, "Children's Deaths Spur Backer of Air Bags to Rethink," *Wall Street Journal*, 18 November 1996, p. A14.
22. ibid.
23. ibid.
24. David B. Ottaway and Warren Brown, "From Life Saver to Threat," *Washington Post*, 1 June 1997, p. A16.
25. ibid.
26. Nomani and Stern, "Children's Deaths Spur Backer of Air Bags to Rethink," p. A14.
27. Ludwig Von Mises, *Human Action* (Chicago: Contemporary Books, [1949]1963), p. 733.

28. Bonnie Liebman and Jayne Hurley, "One Size Doesn't Fit All," *Nutrition Action Healthletter* (Washington, DC: Center for Science in the Public Interest, November 1996), p. 10.

29. Jayne Hurley, Bonnie Liebman, and Stephen Schmidt, "Bad News Breakfasts," *Nutrition Action Healthletter* (Washington, DC: Center for Science in the Public Interest, March 1996), p. 10.

30. Liebman and Hurley, "One Size Doesn't Fit All," p. 10.

31. ibid., pp. 10–11.

32. Rodolfo Acuña and Juana Mora, "Afterword," *Marketing Disease to Hispanics* (Washington, DC: Center for Science in the Public Interest, [1989] 1992), p. 82.

33. ibid., p. 83.

34. Bruce Maxwell and Michael Jacobson, *Marketing Disease to Hispanics*, (Washington, DC: Center for Science in the Public Interest, [1989]1992), p. 23.

35. ibid., p. 49.

36. ibid., p. 77.

37. James M. Buchanan, "Politics and Meddlesome Preferences," in Robert Tollison, ed., *Clearing the Air: Perspectives on Environmental Tobacco Smoke* (Lexington, MA: Lexington Books, 1988), pp. 107–108.

38. Robert Higgs, *Crisis and Leviathan* (New York: Oxford University Press, 1987).

39. James T. Bennett and Thomas J. DiLorenzo, *Official Lies: How Washington Misleads Us* (Alexandria, VA: Groom Books, 1992).

40. Cassandra Chrones Moore, *Haunted Housing: How Toxic Scare Stories Are Spooking the Public Out of House and Home* (Washington, DC: Cato Institute, 1997), p. 257.

41. Malcom Ross, "Foreword," in Cassandra Chrones Moore, *Haunted Housing*, p. xi.

42. Philip K. Howard, *The Death of Common Sense: How Law Is Suffocating America* (New York: Warner Books, 1994).

43. ibid.

Chapter 2

1. Gold, "Damn the Food Police!" p. 53.

2. "No Calendar Girl," *Nutrition Action Healthletter* (Washington, DC: Center for Science in the Public Interest, April 1995), p. 16.

3. "Haagen-Dazs Extra," *Nutrition Action Healthletter* (Washington, DC: Center for Science in the Public Interest, April 1995), p. 9.

4. Jayne Hurley and Stephen Schmidt, "Hard Artery Cafe?" *Nutrition Action Healthletter* (Washington, DC: Center for Science in the Public Interest, October 1996), p. 4.

5. ibid., p. 6.

6. Hurley, Liebman, and Schmidt, "Bad News Breakfasts," p. 9.

7. "Sweets to Die For," *Nutrition Action Healthletter* (Washington, DC: Center for Science in the Public Interest, June 1996), p. 6.

8. Hurley, Liebman, and Schmidt," Bad News Breakfasts," p. 8.

9. Linda Shrieves, "Pendulum Swings Back in Favor of Maligned Egg," *Amarillo Globe-Time (Orlando Sentinel)*, 17 April 1996.

10. Philip E. Ross, "Lies, Damned Lies, and Medical Statistics," *Forbes* (14 August 1995), p. 132.

11. Shrieves, "Pendulum Swings Back in Favor of Maligned Egg."

12. "Tip of the Month," *Nutrition Action Healthletter* (Washington, DC: Center for Science in the Public Interest, June 1996), p. 16.

13. Jayne Hurley and Stephen Schmidt, "Packing the Best Snack," *Nutrition Action*

Healthletter (Washington, DC: Center for Science in the Public Interest, November 1966), p. 8.

14. Shaw, *The Pleasure Police*, p. 87.
15. Jayne Hurley and Stephen Schmidt, "A Wok on the Wild Side," *Nutrition Action Healthletter* (Washington, DC: Center for Science in the Public Interest, September 1993), p. 2.
16. ibid.
17. ibid.
18. ibid.
19. ibid., p. 4.
20. ibid., p. 3.
21. ibid.
22. ibid.
23. Sugarman, "Who Is Michael Jacobson...," p. E4.
24. Daniel Southerland, "Nutrition Study Stirs Ire," *Washington Post*, 5 September 1993, p. B6.
25. Gold, "Damn the Food Police!" p. 54.
26. Jayne Hurley and Stephen Schmidt, "Mexican Food: Oilé," *Nutrition Action Healthletter* (Washington, DC: Center for Science in the Public Interest, July/August 1994), p. 10.
27. ibid.
28. ibid., p. 12.
29. ibid., p. 14.
30. Jayne Hurley and Bonnie Liebman, "When in Rome..." *Nutrition Action Healthletter* (Washington, DC: Center for Science in the Public Interest, January/February 1994), p. 7.
31. ibid., p. 5.
32. ibid., p. 7.
33. Jayne Hurley and Stephen Schmidt, "Movie Theater Snacks," *Nutrition Action Healthletter* (Washington, DC: Center for Science in the Public Interest, May 1994), p. 8.
34. Quoted in Shaw, *The Pleasure Police*, p. 89.
35. Sean Piccoli, "CSPI's 'Food Terrorists' Do Lunch—and It's a Turkey," *Washington Times*, 22 March 1995, pp. A1, A15.
36. Quoted in Klein, *Eat Fat*, p. 61.
37. Quoted in Shaw, *The Pleasure Police*, p. 83.
38. David Schardt and Stephen Schmidt, "Fishing for Safe Seafood," *Nutrition Action Healthletter* (Washington, DC: Center for Science in the Public Interest, November 1996), p. 1.
39. Bonnie Liebman, "Is Seafood a Heart Saver?" *Nutrition Action Healthletter* (Washington, DC: Center for Science in the Public Interest, November 1996), p. 7.
40. Jayne Hurley and Bonnie Liebman, "Seafood: What a Catch," *Nutrition Action Healthletter* (Washington, DC: Center for Science in the Public Interest, November 1996), p. 16.
41. ibid.
42. ibid., p. 17.
43. ibid.
44. Liebman, "Is Seafood a Heart Saver?" p. 6.
45. David Schardt and Stephen Schmidt, "Caffeine: The Inside Scoop," *Nutrition Action Healthletter* (Washington, DC: Center for Science in the Public Interest, December 1996), p. 5.

46. ibid.
47. "Coffee and Cholesterol: Take 18," *Nutrition Action Healthletter* (Washington, DC: Center for Science in the Public Interest, May 1992), p. 4.
48. Shaw, *The Pleasure Police*, p. 87.
49. "Put Down That Carrot," *Women's Fitness & Bodybuilding* (July 1996), p. 4.
50. Daniel Q. Haney, "Junk Food May Be Good for You," Associated Press, 15 May 1996.
51. Randi Hutter Epstein, "Is There a Backlash against Healthy Living?" *Washington Post Health*, 7 January 1997, p. 12.
52. ibid., p. 13.
53. ibid.
54. Nanci Herllmich, "Fat-Free Foods Are Falling Out of Favor with Jilted Dieters," *Rochester Democrat and Chronicle*, 24 February 1997, p. C1.
55. Glenn A. Gaesser, *Big Fat Lies* (New York: Fawcett Columbine, 1996), p. 4.
56. Debbie Johnson, *Think Yourself Thin* (New York: Hyperion, 1996), p. 6.
57. ibid, p. 16.
58. ibid., p. 11.
59. Marilyn Diamond and Dr. Donald Burton Schnell, *Fitonics For Life* (New York: Avon, 1996), p. 34.
60. ibid., p. 35.
61. ibid, p. 155.
62. Neal Barnard, *Eat Right Live Longer* (New York: Harmony, 1995), p. 228.
63. Sheldon Levine, *The Redux Revolution* (New York: Morrow, 1996), p. 12.
64. Adele Puhn, *The 5-Day Miracle Diet* (New York: Ballantine, 1966), p. xi.
65. ibid., p. 8.
66. ibid.
67. Phillip M. Sinaikin with Judith Sachs, *Fat Madness* (New York: Berkley, 1994), p. 3.
68. Gaesser, *Big Fat Lies*, p. ix.
69. ibid., p. xv.
70. ibid., p. 155.
71. Quoted in Laura Fraser, *Losing it: America's Obsession with Weight and the Industry That Feeds on It* (New York: Dutton, 1997), p. 16.
72. Quoted in Gaesser, *Big Fat Lies*, p. 31.
73. Laura Shapiro, "Is Fat That Bad?" *Newsweek* (21 April 1997), p. 64.
74. Gaesser, *Big Fat Lies*, p. 62.
75. ibid., p. 5.
76. ibid.
77. ibid.
78. Shapiro, "Is Fat That Bad?" p. 62.
79. ibid.
80. Shaw, *The Pleasure Police*, pp. 60–61.
81. Gaesser, *Big Fat Lies*, pp. 4–5.
82. ibid., p. 69.
83. ibid., p. 101.
84. ibid., p. 64.
85. Fraser, *Losing It*, p. 285.
86. Quoted in ibid., p. 290.
87. Gaesser, *Big Fat Lies*, p. 81.
88. ibid., p. 82.
89. ibid., p. xvii.
90. Fraser, *Losing It*, p. 176.

91. Quoted in Klein, *Eat Fat*, p. 60.

Chapter 3
1. Quoted in Frank Smallwood, *The Other Candidates: Third Parties in Presidential Elections* (Hanover, NH: University Press of New England, 1983), p. 37.
2. ibid., p. 39.
3. Quoted in Mark Thornton, *The Economics of Prohibition* (Salt Lake City: University of Utah Press, 1993), p. 39.
4. Ian R. Tyrrell, *Sobering Up: From Temperance to Prohibition in Antebellum America* (Westport, CT: Greenwood Press, 1979), p. 4.
5. ibid., p. 135.
6. Quoted in John Kobler, *Ardent Spirits: The Rise and Fall of Prohibition* (New York: G.P. Putnam's Sons, 1973), p. 87.
7. Peter H. Odegard, *Pressure Politics: The Story of the Anti-Saloon League* (New York: Columbia University Press, 1928), p. 245.
8. ibid., p. 38.
9. ibid., p. 39.
10. ibid., p. 42.
11. ibid., p. 66.
12. ibid., p. 42.
13. J.C. Furnas, *The Late Demon Rum* (New York: G.P. Putnam's Sons, 1965), p. 45.
14. ibid., pp. 44–45.
15. Odegard, *Pressure Politics*, p. 40.
16. Kobler, *Ardent Spirits*, p. 143.
17. James H. Timberlake, *Prohibition and the Progressive Movement* (Cambridge, MA: Harvard University Press), p. 50.
18. ibid., p. 53.
19. ibid., p. 27.
20. Odegard, *Pressure Politics*, pp. 157–58.
21. Timberlake, *Prohibition and the Progressive Movement*, p. 80.
22. Furnas, *The Late Demon Rum*, p. 101.
23. Timberlake, *Prohibition and the Progressive Movement*, p. 121.
24. Barbara Jordan, "Preface," *Marketing Booze to Blacks* (Washington, DC: Center for Science in the Public Interest, [1987] 1990), p. ix.
25. George A. Hacker, Ronald Collins, and Michael Jacobson, *Marketing Booze to Blacks*, (Washington, DC: Center for Science in the Public Interest, [1987] 1990), p. xi.
26. ibid., p. 3.
27. ibid., p. 9.
28. ibid., p. 19.
29. ibid., p. 28.
30. ibid., p. 24.
31. ibid., pp. 39–40.
32. ibid., p. xvi.
33. ibid., p. 42.
34. Odegard, *Pressure Politics*, p. 31.
35. ibid., p. 35.
36. Quoted in Mary Bennett Peterson, *The Regulated Consumer* (Ottawa, IL: Green Hill, 1971), p. 34.
37. Odegard, *Pressure Politics*, p. 44.
38. Quoted in Peterson, *The Regulated Consumer*, p. 29.

39. Jack S. Blocker, *Retreat from Reform: The Prohibition Movement in the United States, 1890–1913* (Westport, CT: Greenwood, 1976).
40. E.R. Shipp, "Alcohol Abuse Becomes a Public Policy Issue," *New York Times*, 1 October 1985, p. A1.
41. ibid.
42. "Robert Beck Has Been Driving Force in Mothers Against Drunk Driving," *Wall Street Journal*, 23 August 1990, p. B2.
43. Robert D. McFadden, "Founder of Anti-Drunken Driver Group Loses Two Posts," *New York Times*, 4 October 1985, p. A10.
44. Quoted in Public Interest Profiles, 1992–1993 (Washington, DC: Congressional Quarterly), p. 257.
45. Elizabeth A. Brown, "Alcohol Industry Tries New Image," *Christian Science Monitor*, 19 July 1991, p. 12.
46. Jill Abramson, "Alcohol Industry Is at Forefront of Efforts to Curb Drunkenness," *Wall Street Journal*, 21 May 1991, p. A1.
47. Section 509, Department of Labor, Health and Human Services, and Education and Related Agencies Appropriation Act, 1992, P.L. 102–107, 105 Stat. 1107, 1141 (1991).
48. Doug Bandow, "The Politics of Science, with Federal Grants," *Washington Times*, 15 July 1995, p. C1.
49. U.S. General Accounting Office, "Alleged Lobbying Activities Office for Substance Abuse Prevention," GAO/HRD-93-100 (Washington, DC: GAO, May 1993).
50. "Your Tax Dollars at Work," *Anheuser-Busch Companies Issue Backgrounder* (St. Louis, MO: Anheuser-Busch, no date)
51. Phil Kuntz, "Alcoholic Beverage Industry Lobbies for Bill to Gut Substance Abuse Agency Seen As Threat," *Wall Street Journal*, 14 August 1995, p. A12.
52. Quoted in "Your Tax Dollars at Work," p. 3.
53. Quoted in ibid., p. 4.
54. Jane Lewis Engelke, "Return from the Wilderness," *Commonweal* (26 October 1990), p. 611.
55. "Temperance Group Shifts Attention to Classroom," Associated Press, *Rochester Times-Union*, 17 August 1990.
56. ibid.
57. "'Drink,' Valadimir Said, 'Is the Joy of the Russ,'" Letters, *New York Times*, 27 August 1985.
58. Serge Schmemann, "Soviet Liquor Prices Up in Drive on Alcoholism," *New York Times*, 27 August 1985, p. A6 .
59. William J. Eaton, "Soviet Anti-Alcohol Drive Changing Nation's Habits," *Los Angeles Times*, 26 October 1985, p. 28.
60. Celestine Bohlen, "Crackdown on Drunkenness Is Announced in U.S.S.R.," *Washington Post*, 17 May 1985, p. A26.
61. "Pravda: Soviet Alcohol Sleuths Going Too Far," Associated Press, *Los Angeles Herald-Examiner*, 28 April 1986.
62. ibid.
63. Shipp, "Alcohol Abuse Becomes Public Policy Issue," p. A14.

Chapter 4

1. Bob and Elizabeth Dole, *Unlimited Partners* (New York: Simon and Schuster, 1988), p. 227.
2. Jacob Sullum, "Invasion of the Bottle Snatchers," *Reason* (February 1990), p. 27.

3. Clifford D. May, "Efforts Growing on Drinking Age," *New York Times*, 30 November 1985, p. A1.
4. Thomas J. Knudson, "Drinking Age Is Fiery Issue in West," *New York Times*, 10 March 1987.
5. ibid.
6. Stewart Taylor, Jr., "Justices Are to Consider Suit over Drinking Age," *New York Times*, 2 December 1986.
7. ibid.
8. "Underage Drinking Lurches into the Spotlight," Rochester *Democrat and Chronicle [Washington Post]*, 3 November 1991, p. A18.
9. ibid.
10. Mark Thornton, "Alcohol Prohibition Was a Failure," *CATO Policy Analysis* no. 157 (Washington, DC: Cato Institute, 17 July 1991), p. 6.
11. May, "Efforts Growing on Drinking Age," p. A11.
12. ibid.
13. Elizabeth M. Whelan, "Perils of Prohibition," *Newsweek* (29 May 1995), p. 14.
14. Roderic B. Park, "Creative Alternatives Needed; A 'Learner's Permit' for Drinking?" *Washington Post*, 9 December 1996, p. C1.
15. May, "Efforts Growing on Drinking Age," p. A11.
16. Quoted in Fredric N. Bolotin and Jack DeSario, "The Politics and Policy Implications of a National Minimum Drinking Age," unpublished ms., Cleveland, OH, Case Western Reserve University, p. 5. Also, see Fredric N. Bolotin and Jack DeSario, "Raising the Drinking Age Won't Work," *Consumer's Research Magazine* 69 (July 1986), pp. 11–17.
17. Quoted in ibid., p. 12.
18. ibid.
19. Jack P. DeSario and Fredric N. Bolotin, "A Sober Look at a Drunken Driving Cure-All," *Wall Street Journal*, 31 December 1985, editorial page.
20. ibid.
21. ibid.
22. William Bole, "Trend Is to Moderate Alcohol Use," *Western New York Catholic Visitor* (December 1983).
23. Jesus Rangel, "Bill to Curb 'Happy Hours' at Bars Arouses Debate," *New York Times*, 17 February 1985, p. 41.
24. Michael J. McCarthy, "For Finding Loopholes in the Law, There's Just No Place Like Kansas," *Wall Street Journal*, 18 November 1985.
25. J. Michael Kennedy, "26 States Still Think Joe Six-Pack Has a Right to Swig while He Drives," *Rochester Democrat and Chronicle [Los Angeles Times]*, 27 January 1985, p. 7A.
26. ibid.
27. Dale M. Heien, "Are Higher Alcohol Taxes Justified?" *CATO Journal* 15 (Fall/Winter 1995/96), pp. 243–57.
28. Doug Bandow, "Drunken Driving Standards in Flux," *Washington Times*, 22 February 1993, p. E3.
29. David W. Moore and R. Kelly Myers, "Strategies to Reduce Drink Driving: A National Survey" (Washington, DC: American Beverage Institute, 2 August 1992), p. 1.
30. ibid., p. 3.
31. Sullum, "Invasion of the Bottle Snatchers," p. 29.
32. "Jailing Drunk Drivers: Impact on the Criminal Justice System," *National Institute of Justice Reports* (Washington, DC: U.S. Department of Justice, July 1985), p. 2.

33. ibid.
34. ibid., p. 4.
35. Nicholas von Hoffman, "Some of Those Horror Stories in the Press Are Just Hot Air," *Los Angeles Herald-Examiner*, 17 July 1985.
36. *Public Interest Profiles*, 1992–1993, p. 258.
37. Heien, "Are Higher Alcohol Taxes Justified?"
38. "Drunk Driving: A Killer We Can Stop" (New York: Insurance Information Institute, 1983).
39. Shaw, *The Pleasure Police*, p. 112.
40. ibid., pp. 112–13.
41. George A. Hacker and Michael F. Jacobson, "Higher Taxes Save Lives and Cut Abuse," *New York Times*, 25 May 1986.
42. ibid.
43. "CSPI Alcohol Policies Project" (pamphlet) (Washington, DC: Center for Science in the Public Interest, no date).
44. "State Alcohol Taxes and Health: A Citizen's Action Guide," Preface (Washington, DC: Center for Science in the Public Interest, 1996).
45. Gary Klott, "...And It Might Cost More to Drink, Smoke and Drive," *New York Times*, 7 May 1987, p. D20.
46. ibid.
47. Shipp, "Alcohol Abuse Becomes a Public Policy Issue."
48. ibid.
49. Heien, "Are Higher Alcohol Taxes Justified?"
50. ibid.
51. Thornton, "Alcohol Prohibition Was a Failure," p. 1.
52. "Alcohol Can Aid Blood Flow," Associated Press, *Rochester Democrat and Chronicle*, 4 February 1997.
53. "Group Finds Compound in Grapes That Inhibits Growth of Cancer," Associated Press, 10 January 1997.
54. Shaw, *The Pleasure Police*, p. 119.
55. Quoted in ibid., p. 118.
56. "More Wining," Rochester *Democrat and Chronicle*, 31 March 1997, p. C1.
57. "Prohibition Party Platform 1996," pamphlet.

Chapter 5

1. Shaw, *The Pleasure Police*, p. 116.
2. Ben Lieberman, "The Power of Positive Drinking," *CEI Update* (Washington, DC: Competitive Enterprise Institute, November 1996), p. 1.
3. Donna K.H. Walters, "Tag Telling of Wine Benefits Uncorks Anger," *Los Angeles Times*, 24 October 1992, p. A27.
4. ibid.
5. Lieberman, "The Power of Positive Drinking," p. 8.
6. ibid.
7. "A National Survey of Public Knowledge Regarding the Health Benefits of Moderate Alcohol Consumption," (Washington, DC: Competitive Enterprise Institute, November, 1995).
8. "Institute Wines for Free Speech," press release (Washington, DC: Competitive Enterprise Institute, 8 May 1995).
9. Letter of James R. Crandall to Frances B. Smith, 24 October 1995.
10. Quoted in *Competitive Enterprise Institute and Consumer Alert v. Robert E. Rubin and John W. Magaw*, United States District Court for the District of Columbia, 29 October 1996, p. 6.

11. "Health Experts Criticize Effort to Encourage 'Moderate' Drinking as Official U.S. Policy," press release (Washington, DC: Center for Science in the Public Interest, no date).
12. Quoted in Sullum, "Invasion of the Bottle Snatchers," p. 28.
13. ibid.
14. Quoted in "Broadcast Liquor Ad Protests Continue," *Boozenews* Action Alert (Washington, DC: Center for Science in the Public Interest, September 1996).
15. Coalition for the Prevention of Alcohol Problems, *Action Alert* (Washington, DC: CPAP, November 1996).
16. Sullum, "Invasion of the Bottle Snatchers," p. 32.
17. "What You Can Do to Support Health and Safety Warning Messages in Alcohol Ads," Coalition on Alcohol Advertising and Family Education (Washington, DC: CAAFE, April 1991), p. 12.
18. "Alcohol Advertising Facts," (Washington, DC: Center for Science in the Public Interest, no date).
19. ibid.
20. "Talking Points/Arguments to Stop Seagram's Broadcase Liquor Ads," Coalition for the Prevention of Alcohol Problems (Washington, DC: CPAP, November 1996).
21. "What You Can Do to Support Health and Safety Warning Messages in Alcohol Ads," p. 6.
22. ibid., p. 13.
23. Michael F. Jacobson and Ronald Collins, "Ads Glamorize Alcohol, Hide Dangers," *New York Times*, 21 April 1985, p. C2.
24. Sullum, "Invasion of the Bottle Snatchers," p. 32.
25. James Bovard, "The Second Murder of Crazy Horse," *Wall Street Journal*, 15 September 1992, p. A16.
26. ibid.
27. "Testimony of William T. Earle before the Select Committee on Children, Youth, and Families," 19 May 1992, p. 3.
28. ibid., p. 4.
29. "Antonia C. Novello, Testimony on Crazy Horse Malt Liquor before the House Select Committee on Children, Youth, and Families," 19 May 1992, p. 3.
30. ibid., p. 5.
31. Quoted in "Opening Statement, Patricia Schroeder, Select Committee on Children, Youth, and Families," 19 May 1992, p. 2.
32. Novello, Testimony, p. 4.
33. "Testimony of Gregg Bourland before the Select Committee on Children, Youth, and Families," 19 May 1992, p. 1.
34. ibid., p. 3.
35. "Prepared Statement of Robert A. Destro before the Select Committee on Children, Youth, and Families," 19 May 1992, p. 6.
36. Bovard, "The Second Murder of Crazy Horse."
37. David Kessler, "We've Fought the Good Fight," *Newsweek* (9 December 1996), p. 28.
38. "The Commish under Fire," *Time* (8 January 1996), p. 60.
39. Peterson, *The Regulated Consumer*, p. 50.
40. Quoted in Justus D. Doenecke, *Not to the Swift: The Old Isolationists in the Cold War Era* (Lewisburg, PA: Bucknell, 1979), p. 217.
41. Peterson, *The Regulated Consumer*, p. 41
42. ibid., p. 42.
43. "Court Requires Restaurant Menus to Meet FDA Standards for Health and Nu-

trition Claims," press release (Washington, DC: Center for Science in the Public Interest, 2 July 1996).

44. Mary MacVean, "Vitamins, Herbs Regulation Battle Looming," Associated Press, 2 June 1993.
45. ibid.
46. ibid.
47. "The Commish under Fire," p. 47.
48. Durk Pearson and Sandy Shaw, *Freedom of Informed Choice: FDA Versus Nutrient Supplements* (Neptune, NJ: Common Sense Press, 1993), p. 1.
49. Sandy Shaw, "Take Half an Aspirin and Call Me in Four Years," *Liberty* (January 1997).
50. Quoted in ibid.
51. Pearson and Shaw, *Freedom of Informed Choice*, p. 8.
52. Kenneth Lee, "Republicans, Drug Money, and You," *Liberty* (March 1997), p. 45.
53. Quoted in ibid., p. 46.

Chapter 6

1. "Total Nutrition," *Nutrition Action Healthletter* (Washington, DC: Center for Science in the Public Interest, June 1996), p. 15.
2. Michael D. Limonick, "Are We Ready for Fat-Free Fat?" *Time* (8 January 1996), p. 53.
3. ibid.
4. American Dietetic Association, "Review of ADA Position on Fat Replacements," (Chicago, IL: ADA, approved 10 November 1995).
5. Paula Kurtzweil, "Taking the Fat out of Food," *FDA Consumer* (July-August 1996), p. 13.
6. Keith C. Triebwasser, "Speaker Notes Used at FAC [Food Advisory Committee of the FDA] Meeting," November 1995, p. 12.
7. "FDA Approves Fat Substitute, Olestra," *HHS News*, 24 January 1996, p. 3.
8. Myra Karstadt and Stephen Schmidt, "Olestra: Procter's Big Gamble," *Nutrition Action Healthletter* (Washington, DC: Center for Science in the Public Interest, March 1996), p. 4.
9. Limonick, "Are We Ready for Fat-Free Fat?" p. 58.
10. Nora Zorich, "Speaker Notes Used at FAC [Food Advisory Committee of the FDA] Meeting," p. 15.
11. ibid., p. 33.
12. "FDA Approves Fat Substitute, Olestra," p. 2.
13. "CSPI Throws Consumer Choice Down the Toilet, Says Consumer Alert," press release (Washington, DC: Consumer Alert, 1 July 1996).
14. John Berlau, "Cursing the Cure for Fatty Food," *Washington Times*, 11 July 1996, p. A15.
15. Glass, "Hazardous to Your Mental Health," p. 20.
16. Michael F. Jacobson, Press Conference on Olestra, 1 July 1996, p. 2.
17. ibid.
18. "Case Histories," CSPI press release (Washington, DC: Center for Science in the Public Interest, 1 July 1996), p.3.
19. Michael F. Jacobson, Press Conference, p. 3.
20. Bruskin Goldring Research, "Max Chips—Market Research Study," (Edison, NJ: BGR, 27 June 1996), p. 2.
21. Glass, "Hazardous to Your Mental Health," p. 20.
22. Diamond and Schnell, *Fitonics for Life*, p. 162.

23. "So, How Does It Taste?" *Time* (8 January 1996), p. 59.

24. Glass, "Hazardous to Your Mental Health," p. 19.

25. ibid, p. 19.

26. Karstadt and Schmidt, "Olestra, Procter's Big Gamble," p. 4.

27. Glass, "Hazardous to Your Mental Health," p. 19.

28. "Olestra Is a Good Way to Reduce Fat Intake," Letters, *New York Times*, 26 May 1996, p. D10.

29. Karstadt and Schmidt, "Olestra: Procter's Big Gamble," p. 4.

30. Glass, "Hazardous to Your Mental Health," p. 20.

31. "In Point of Fact," *World Health Organization*, no. 40, 1987.

32. American Spice Trade Association, "What Consumers Really Think about Irradiated Foods," (Englewood Cliffs, NJ: ASTA, n.d.), p. 3.

33. "Safety and Nutritional Adequacy of Irradiated Food: *WHO* Publishs a Comprehensive Study," *WHO* Press Release (Washington, DC: World Health Organization, 13 October 1994), p. 2.

34. "Food Irradiation: Added Value Not Risk," *WHO* Press Release (Washington, DC: World Health Organization, 27 May 1992), p. 2.

35. "Dishing Up Gamma Rays," *Newsweek* (27 January 1992), p. 52.

36. Colman Andres, "Happy Birthday, Julia!" *Metropolitan Home* (September 1992), p. 47.

37. Nation's Pride, "Increase Sales with Fresh Irradiated Produce" (Plant City, FL: Nation's Pride, n.d.).

38. Donald W. Thayer et al., "Radiation Pasteurization of Food," *Cast Issue Paper* (Ames, IA: Council for Agricultural Science and Technology, April 1996), p. 3.

39. "Radiation-Exposed Beef: It's What's NOT for Dinner," (Marshfield, VT: Food & Water, Inc., n.d.).

40. *20/20*, ABC News, 27 January 1993.

41. ibid.

42. "Radiation—Exposed Food," Text of National Radio Advertisement, Food & Water Incorporated, 1990.

43. Bruce Ingersoll, "Schwartz Disavows Ad Denouncing Food Irradiation," *Wall Street Journal* in "The Media Story of Food Irradiation" (Kanata, Ont., Canada: Nordion International, July 1996).

44. Letter of Michael Colby, Food & Water, Inc., 31 May 1996.

45. Quoted in John Berlau, "Irradiation, Not More Regulation, for Greater Food Safety," *Consumer Alert Issue Brief* (Washington, DC: Consumer Alert, n.d.).

46. American Spice Trade Association, "What Consumers Really Think about Irradiated Food," p. 3.

47. American Meat Institute, "The More Consumers Learn about Irradiation, the More They Want It," News Release (Washington, DC: AMI, 7 October 1993), p. 2.

48. Larry Katzenstein, "Good Food You Can't Get," *Reader's Digest* (July 1993), p. 47.

49. Tony Hiss, "How Now, Drugged Cow?" *Harper's* (October 1994), p. 81.

50. Quoted in *International Dairy Foods Association et al. v. Jeffrey Amestoy and Leon C. Graves*, United States Court of Appeals for the Second Circuit, 8 August 1996, Docket no. 95-7819, p. 11.

51. Food & Water, Inc., "Urgent BGH Action Alert!" (Marshfield, VT: F&W, n.d.).

52. Jeremy Rifkin, Letter to David Kessler, 29 November 1990, pp. 2–3. Emphasis added.

53. Bruce Ingersoll, "Use of Growth Hormone in Milk Cows Is Assailed by Two Consumer Groups," *Wall Street Journal*, 4 December 1990, p. B3.

54. Hiss, "How Now, Drugged Cow?" p. 81.
55. ibid, p. 82.
56. ibid.
57. ibid.
58. Letter of John Berlau to *Harper's*, 31 October 1994.
59. Larry Katzenstein, "Consumers Union Credibility—Good But Slipping," *Wall Street Journal*, 8 August 1994, editorial page.
60. William H. Daughaday and David M. Barbano, "Bovine Somatotropin Supplementation of Dairy Cows," *Journal of the American Medical Association* (22/29 August 1990), pp. 1003–1004.
61. Docket 95-7819, p. 3.
62. Hiss, "How Now, Drugged Cow?" p. 81.
63. ibid.
64. Charles J. Grossman, "Genetic Engineering and the Use of Bovine Somatotropin," *Journal of the American Medical Association* (22/29 August 1990), p. 1028.
65. Letter of John Berlau to *Harper's*, p. 1.
66. ibid., pp. 1–2.
67. Grossman, "Genetic Engineering and the Use of Bovine Somatotropin," p. 1028.
68. Katzenstein, "Consumers Union Credibility—Good but Slipping."
69. Ingersoll, "Use of Growth Hormone in Milk Cows Is Assailed by Two Consumer Groups."

Chapter 7

 1. Quoted in Ronald Bailey, "Fear and Loathing of Biotech's Bright Future," *Reason* (November 1985), p. 25.
 2. ibid.
 3. ibid., p. 26.
 4. Michael Fritz, "Thank You, Jeremy Rifkin," *Forbes* (16 October 1989), p. 269.
 5. Larry Thompson, "Poll Finds Support for Use of Gene Therapy," *Washington Post*, 25 September 1990, p. Z9.
 6. Marlene Cimons, "Human Gene Therapy Test Receives Key U.S. Approval," *Los Angeles Times*, 1 August 1990, p. A1.
 7. Bailey, "Fear and Loathing of Biotech's Future," p. 24.
 8. ibid.
 9. Cimons, "Human Gene Therapy Test Receives Key U.S. Approval."
10. Fritz, "Thank You, Jeremy Rifkin," p. 268.
11. ibid.
12. Bailey, "Fear and Loathing of Biotech's Bright Future," p. 28.
13. ibid., p. 23.
14. ibid., p. 28.
15. ibid., p. 29.
16. Recombinant DNA Advisory Committee, minutes of meeting, 30 January 1989, p. 11.
17. ibid., p. 32.
18. Mike Royko, "Eco-Nags…In Your Windshield," *Washington Times*, 22 November 1992, editorial page.
19. ibid.
20. Thompson, "Poll Finds Support for Use of Gene Therapy."
21. Ronald Bailey, "Ministry of Fear," *Forbes*, 27 June 1988, p. 138.
22. ibid., p. 139.
23. Bailey, "Fear and Loathing of Biotech's Bright Future," p. 22.
24. ibid., p. 30.

25. Bailey, "Ministry of Fear," p. 139.
26. Jeremy Rifkin, *Beyond Beef* (New York: Dutton, 1992), p. 1.
27. ibid., p. 2.
28. ibid.
29. ibid.
30. ibid., p. 4.
31. ibid., p. 51.
32. ibid., p. 32.
33. ibid.
34. ibid., p. 35.
35. ibid., p. 63.
36. ibid., p. 64.
37. ibid., p. 154.
36. ibid.
39. ibid., p. 156.
40. ibid., p. 239.
41. ibid., p. 244.
42. ibid., pp. 260–61.
43. ibid., p. 268.
44. Colman McCarthy, "The High Price of Hamburger," *Washington Post Book Review*, 31 May 1992.
45. Rifkin, *Beyond Beef*, p. 284.
46. National Cattlemen's Association, "Industry Facts: Resource Use," *Cattle and Beef Handbook* (Englewood, CO: NCA, 1992).
47. Tom Jackson, "Our Environment," *Better Homes and Gardens* (August 1992), p. 94.
48. Dennis Avery, "Beefing Up the Diet Diatribe," *Hudson Opinion* (Indianapolis, IN: Hudson Institute, March 1993), p. 3.
49. Malcolm Gladwell, "'Beyond Beef' Ad Campaign Set to Begin," *Washington Post*, 15 April 1992, p. A20.
50. Rifkin, *Beyond Beef*, p. 159.
51. ibid., p. 160.
52. ibid., p. 59.
53. ibid., p. 99.
54. ibid., p. 163.
55. ibid., p. 181.
56. ibid., p. 176.
57. ibid., p. 185.
58. ibid., p. 186.
59. National Cattlemen's Association, "Myths and Facts about Beef Production" (Englewood, CO: NCA, n.d.), p. 4.
60. Rifkin, *Beyond Beef*, p. 4.
61. National Cattlemen's Association, "Industry Facts: Remarkable Ruminants" (Englewood, CO: NCA, n.d.).
62. Rifkin, *Beyond Beef*, p. 242.
63. ibid., p. 165.
64. ibid., p. 169.
65. ibid., p. 175.
66. National Cattlemen's Association, "References: Beef in the Diet," *Cattle and Beef Handbook* (Englewood, CO: NCA, 1992), p. 7.
67. Carole Sugarman, "Beefing about the American Diet," *Washington Post*, 28 April 1991.

68. ibid.
69. National Cattlemen's Association, "Industry Facts: Beef in the Diet," *Cattle and Beef Handbook* (Englewood, CO: NCA, 1992), p. 1.
70. ibid., p. 4.
71. Liebman, "A Dozen Dos & Don'ts," p. 11.
72. Carole Sugarman, "Labels about Safe Handling to be Required on Meat, Poultry Products," *Washington Post,* 12 August 1993, p. A3.
73. Sugarman, "Beefing about the American Diet."
74. Letters, *Washington Post Book Review*, 12 July 1992, p. 14.

Chapter 8

1. Klein, *Eat Fat*, p. 93.
2. Quoted in Klein, *Eat Fat*, p. 195.
3. Kelly D. Brownell, "Get Slim with Higher Taxes," *New York Times*, 15 December 1994, p. A29.
4. ibid.
5. Klein, *Eat Fat*, p. 196.
6. Brownell, "Get Slim with Higher Taxes."
7. Jacqueline Weaver, "Americans, Obesity and Eating Habits," *New York Times*, 29 January 1995.
8. Bole, "Trend Is to Moderate Alcohol Use."
9. Henry David Thoreau, *Walden* (New York: New American Library, [1854]1960), pp. 106–107.
10. Friedrich Hayek, *The Constitution of Liberty* (Chicago: University of Chicago Press, 1960), p. 71.
11. ibid., pp. 71–72.
12. Charles Murray, *In Pursuit: Of Happiness and Good Government* (New York: Basic Books, 1989).
13. Israel Kirzner, *Discovery and the Capitalist Process* (Chicago: University of Chicago Press, 1985), p. 130.
14. ibid., p. 144.
15. Alan Greenspan, "The Assault on Integrity," in Ayn Rand, ed., *Capitalism: The Unknown Ideal* (New York: Signet, 1967), p. 118.
16. ibid., p. 120.

Index